MW00642226

ANGELS

ANGELS

AGENTS *of* LIGHT, LOVE, AND POWER

DONALD W. PARRY

DESERET
BOOK

Salt Lake City, Utah

To my beloved Camille and our six children—

Matthew, Julie, Justin, Kirkham, Stephen, and Rachel

"Happy is the man" (Psalm 127:5)

© 2013 Donald W. Parry

All rights reserved. No part of this book may be reproduced in any form or by any means without permission in writing from the publisher, Deseret Book Company, at permissions@ deseretbook.com or P. O. Box 30178, Salt Lake City, Utah 84130. This work is not an official publication of The Church of Jesus Christ of Latter-day Saints. The views expressed herein are the responsibility of the author and do not necessarily represent the position of the Church or of Deseret Book Company.

DESERET BOOK is a registered trademark of Deseret Book Company.

Visit us at DeseretBook.com

First printing in hardbound 2013
First printing in paperbound 2015

Library of Congress Cataloging-in-Publication Data

Parry, Donald W., author.
    Angels : agents of light, love, and power / Donald W. Parry.
       pages cm
    Includes bibliographical references and index.
    ISBN 978-1-60907-519-4 (hardbound : alk. paper)
    ISBN 978-1-62972-075-3 (paperbound)
    1. Angels—The Church of Jesus Christ of Latter-day Saints. 2. The Church of Jesus Christ of Latter-day Saints—Doctrines. 3. Mormon Church—Doctrines. I. Title.
    BT966.3.P37 2013
    235'.3—dc23   2013014165

Printed in the United States of America
RR Donnelley, Harrisonburg, VA

10 9 8 7 6 5 4 3

CONTENTS

CONTENTS

PREFACE

As I have studied the scriptures and the words of latter-day prophets and apostles, I have become impressed with just how many of those prophets and apostles—ancient and modern—have spoken or written about angels. Because this volume deals chiefly with the Lord's angels, not Satan and his minions, every reference to angels, whether one or more, deals with the Lord's angels, unless stated explicitly otherwise.

This volume does not contain an exhaustive discussion of the subject of the Lord's angels. To avoid sensationalism and untrue or misleading notions regarding angels, with only a few exceptions I have limited the sources used here to ancient and modern scripture and the teachings of apostles and prophets in this dispensation. My rule was to find and provide here multiple sources from prophets or apostles regarding angels. Any exceptions are carefully documented sources or accounts that are aligned with the teachings of general authorities of the Church.

I have approached the topic with caution. Many teachings regarding angels must remain tentative and provisional because there is so much we do not know; we must ever remain humble and teachable. Perhaps the Lord's revelation regarding the Apocrypha can apply to teachings about angels: "Therefore, whoso readeth it, let him understand, for the Spirit manifesteth truth; and whoso is enlightened by the Spirit shall obtain benefit therefrom" (D&C 91:4–5).

Some statements and accounts of angels, even though they may have been published and widely distributed, are not doctrine. The world offers documentaries, nonfictional writings, television programs, movies, fictional works, and much more on the subject of angels. How should readers understand such teachings? If they are not aligned with the teachings of our prophets and apostles, they do not belong in any meaningful discussion of angels.

When we read accounts of angels that seem to contain symbols—such as angels with swords, chariots, trumpets, or keys—we must remain tentative in our interpretation of those symbols. We do not always know when such swords, chariots, trumpets, or keys are literal, or symbolic, or both literal and symbolic. I have treated these symbols with caution and watchfulness.

Many of the quotations in this volume come from nineteenth century sources, whose punctuation, syntax, spelling, and capitalization were more individual. For ease of reading by modern readers, I have usually standardized punctuation, syntax, spelling, and capitalization.

I have occasionally used in this volume translations of the Bible other than the King James Version (KJV), when that other translation provided insight into the meaning of individual words or passages: American Standard Version (ASV) and the Joseph Smith Translation (JST).

ACKNOWLEDGMENTS

I am indebted to all whose efforts have made this book possible. In particular, I am grateful to Cory Maxwell, director of publishing at Deseret Book Company, for his continual encouragement, support, and guidance, and to Suzanne Brady, managing editor, who worked tirelessly, with both competence and professionalism, to fine-tune the manuscript and oversee its preparation for press. I also gratefully acknowledge Rachael Ward, typographer; Shauna Gibby, designer; and proofreaders Kalina Lowery and Ruth Howard.

I extend deep appreciation to professor Brent L. Top, chair of the Department of Church History and Doctrine, Brigham Young University, for reading the entire manuscript and making many helpful suggestions. I thank Amanda Taylor and Jared Pfost, who served well in conducting the source-checking efforts for this volume; they examined more than three hundred footnotes that accompany the body of the text.

And I will be eternally thankful to my parents, Atwell and Elaine Parry, for teaching me to love the sacred word of God, as revealed to both ancient and modern prophets and apostles.

WE BELIEVE IN THE MINISTRY OF ANGELS

*I believe we need to speak of and
believe in and bear testimony of the ministry
of angels more than we sometimes do.*

ELDER JEFFREY R. HOLLAND

An angel from another sphere came to planet Earth, our modest little planet in a vast assembly of galaxies and constellations; he came to a young prophet who lived in a humble home near an inconspicuous village. This angel knew where Joseph Smith lived, he spoke English, and he knew Joseph's name. Moreover, this angel apparently did not enter through a door or window; he stood "in the air," wore a robe of "most exquisite whiteness," and filled the room with light until it was "lighter than at noonday." This angel's "whole person was glorious beyond description." Furthermore, he cited scriptures from ancient prophets from our very own planet Earth. This angel's name was Moroni (an unusual name to a frontier boy). Moroni's exit from the Prophet's home was as dramatic as his entry. After delivering

"For a Wise Purpose," *Ensign*, Jan. 1996, 17.

his message, he ascended in "a conduit open right up into heaven" (Joseph Smith–History 1:30–33, 36–41, 43).

Who was this angel? He was God's messenger, sent from God's presence. When did he make his appearance? On September 21, 1823.

How remarkable and how wonderful is this account, which is not only captivating but also sacred. It makes me joyful and draws me closer to my Heavenly Father. Who is not spiritually affected when reading this account with an open heart?

On account of his visits to Joseph Smith, this angel is well-known to Latter-day Saints and others. A statue representing Moroni stands prominently on top of scores of LDS temples throughout the world. Book of Mormon introductory pages feature the account of Moroni's visits to Joseph Smith—and millions of copies of the Book of Mormon have been distributed among many peoples and nations. Tens of thousands of full-time missionaries have testified to investigators regarding Moroni's visits to Joseph Smith. I, too, have testified, again and again, to many individuals, families, and groups of the truth of Moroni's visit to Joseph.

Another scriptural passage about an angel affected me so greatly that I memorized it when I was a teenager: "And I saw another angel fly in the midst of heaven" (Revelation 14:6). Many Church leaders have associated this passage with Moroni. President Gordon B. Hinckley, for example, said plainly: "John the Revelator 'saw another angel fly in the midst of heaven, having the everlasting gospel to preach unto them that dwell on the earth, and to every nation, and kindred, and tongue, and people' (Revelation 14:6). That angel has come. His name is Moroni."[1]

Other scriptural passages about angels have also influenced me—the angel who saved Daniel from peril when he was cast to the lions; the angel who appeared to Mary, the mother of Jesus; and the angel John the Baptist, who restored the Aaronic Priesthood.

Angels play a prominent part in the Lord's plan of salvation in all dispensations, and our own dispensation is no exception. In fact, our dispensation has been a period of extraordinary angelic activity. Joseph Smith received dozens of communications from angels. The Church of Jesus Christ of Latter-day Saints was restored, in part, through angels' imparting revelations and truths to the Prophet Joseph Smith.

In our own dispensation, prophets and apostles have testified of the eminence and considerable standing of angels. Church authorities in all the years since Joseph Smith have taught a great deal about angels. During the decades since 1971, general conference speakers have referred to angels or cited scriptures about angels more than fourteen hundred times. Church leaders have also referred to angels in other settings; those teachings are published in the *Ensign* magazine, Conference Reports, and other official Church publications. These teachings have blessed me in numerous ways, because they instruct me regarding the momentous activities of angels among mortals.

When we talk about such angels as Moroni or John the

---

1. "Stay the Course—Keep the Faith," *Ensign,* Nov. 1995, 70.

Baptist, we often think of the early days of the . . . Restoration and of . . . individuals such as Joseph Smith and Oliver Cowdery. In other words, we may consider that we who live in the twenty-first century are far removed from such angelic activities. But let's put the matter on a personal level. Elder Jeffrey R. Holland wrote these significant words: "One of the things that will become more important in our lives the longer we live is the reality of angels, their work and their ministry. I refer here not alone to the angel Moroni but also to those more personal ministering angels who are with us and around us, empowered to help us and who do exactly that."[2]

I love those words, uttered by one of the Lord's special witnesses. They speak directly to me. Without a doubt there are "personal ministering angels," as Elder Holland testifies. They are "with us and around us." And they are "empowered to help us."

Now, in the present day, during our mortal probation, angels personally affect each one of us who partakes of the blessings of the gospel because they restored priesthood keys and rights that enable us to receive various ordinances, including the blessings of baptism, the sacrament, temple marriage, and the sealing of families. Also, because of these priesthood keys, which were restored by angels, we derive untold spiritual benefits from receiving the gift of the Holy Ghost. Furthermore, because of the divine work of angels in this dispensation—

- We are privileged to have the Book of Mormon.
- Our little children sometimes enjoy unique spiritual privileges.

---

2. "For a Wise Purpose," *Ensign*, Jan. 1996, 16–17.

- Angels may administer love, comfort, or peace to us.
- Angels may communicate with us through a visitation, a voice, by thoughts, by feelings, or in other ways.
- Angels are coworkers with us in missionary service.
- Angels assist us as we conduct work for the dead.
- Angels conduct divine work among the nations in our day, in preparation for the Second Coming.
- Angels will accompany Jesus Christ at his second coming.
- And there is much more.

In sum, angelic activities in this dispensation have personal application to each one of us who is sincerely seeking to live the gospel.

It is my testimony that angels do exist, that they appeared to the Prophet Joseph Smith, and that they were sent by the Lord to restore keys, rights, and authority to him. I testify also that the sacred work of angels continues in our own time. I am convinced that angels are at work among us now.

Chapter 1

WHAT ARE ANGELS?

❧❧❧ ❦❦❦

*Gods, angels and men are all of one
species, one race, one great family, widely
diffused among the planetary systems.*

ELDER PARLEY P. PRATT

What are angels? Because numerous misconceptions exist regarding angels, let us examine what we know from scripture and the teachings of latter-day prophets and apostles.

- Angels are the offspring of God.
- Angels operate among men, women, and children.
- Angels do not have wings.
- Angels are messengers.
- Angels who minister on this earth have belonged to it or may yet belong to it.
- Angels are our fellow servants in the work of the Lord.
- Angels may be males or females.
- Angels have the form of men or women.
- Angels are organized into classes.

Key to the Science of Theology, 33.

ANGELS ARE THE OFFSPRING OF GOD

Angels are children of our Heavenly Father. President Joseph F. Smith explained, "When messengers are sent to minister to the inhabitants of this earth, they are not strangers, but from the ranks of our kindred, friends, and fellow-beings and fellow-servants."[1] And Elder Parley P. Pratt wrote that "Gods, angels and men are all of one species, one race, one great family, widely diffused among the planetary systems, as colonies, kingdoms, nations, &c."[2]

ANGELS OPERATE AMONG MEN, WOMEN, AND CHILDREN

Angels do not restrict their appearances or communications to a particular gender, age group, tribe, or nation; rather, angels operate among all humankind—men, women, and children— according to the Lord's divine will (see LDS Bible Dictionary). Alma 32:23 states that God "imparteth his word by angels unto men, yea, not only men but women also. Now this is not all; little children do have words given unto them many times, which confound the wise and the learned." Joseph Smith's promise to members of the Relief Society—"If you live up to your privileges, the angels cannot be restrained from being your associates"[3]—may also apply to men and children.

ANGELS DO NOT HAVE WINGS

The Prophet Joseph Smith taught, "An angel of God never

---

1. *Gospel Doctrine*, 435.
2. *Key to the Science of Theology*, 33; see also Smith, *Gospel Doctrine*, 112.
3. *History of the Church*, 4:605.

has wings."[4] The widely held notion that angels have wings originated from several sources.

First, the scriptures set forth that seraphs (Hebrew, *seraphim*) have wings (see Isaiah 6:2). Ezekiel (Ezekiel 1:9–11) and John (Revelation 4:8) envisioned living creatures with wings; these wings are probably not literal but, rather, symbolic of angels' abilities to move about. In fact, when the Prophet Joseph inquired about this subject, he received the answer that the wings are a "representation of power, to move, to act, etc." (D&C 77:4).

Second, artists continue to perpetuate the idea that angels have wings. President George Q. Cannon explained: "The early artists, long centuries ago, are credited with the idea of painting angels with wings. . . . From that time to the present this has been accepted as the proper form in which to present angels. It has become a firmly fixed tradition in the Christian world that angels must have wings."[5]

ANGELS ARE MESSENGERS

The English word *angel* is from a Greek word (*angelos*) that means "messenger." Likewise, the Hebrew word *malakh*, usually translated "angel," also signifies "messenger." President Charles W. Penrose explained, "Angels are God's messengers, whether used in that capacity as unembodied spirits, selected according to their capacities for the work required, or as disembodied spirits, or as translated men, or as resurrected beings."[6]

---

4. *Teachings of the Prophet Joseph Smith*, 162.
5. *Gospel Truth*, 1:69.
6. "Who and What Are the Angels," *Improvement Era* 15 (Aug. 1912): 950.

As messengers, angels deliver a variety of messages to mortals—messages of love, comfort, warning, or admonition. Further, angels teach the gospel, declare repentance, explain doctrine, and restore priesthood, keys, powers, authority, and more. Angels' messages may be spoken or unspoken or felt, or they may come by some other means.

ANGELS WHO MINISTER ON THIS EARTH HAVE BELONGED TO IT OR MAY YET BELONG TO IT

Doctrine and Covenants 130:4–5 states: "In answer to the question—Is not the reckoning of God's time, angel's time, prophet's time, and man's time, according to the planet on which they reside? I answer, Yes. But there are no angels who minister to this earth but those who do belong or have belonged to it." Accordingly, the well-known angels Michael, Gabriel, John the Baptist, Peter, James, John, Moroni, and many others are historical persons who have lived upon this earth. Other angels who have ministered on this earth may have done so before they were born in the flesh.

ANGELS ARE OUR FELLOW SERVANTS IN THE WORK OF THE LORD

When the angel John the Baptist ordained Joseph Smith and Oliver Cowdery, he spoke the words, "Upon you my fellow servants" (D&C 13:1). Similarly, the angel who instructed John the Revelator told him, "I am thy fellowservant, and of thy brethren that have the testimony of Jesus" (Revelation 19:10) and later said, "I am thy fellowservant, and of thy brethren the prophets" (Revelation 22:9).

ANGELS MAY BE MALES OR FEMALES

Although male angels—for example, Michael, Gabriel, John the Baptist, Peter, James, John, and others—figure prominently in texts that pertain to the restoration of the gospel, priesthood, and keys, female angels certainly exist. Brigham Young said: "Suppose that a female angel were to come into your house and you had the privilege of seeing her, how would she be dressed? . . . She would be neat and nice, her countenance full of glory, brilliant, bright, and perfectly beautiful, and in every act her gracefulness would charm the heart of every beholder. There is nothing needless about her."[7]

ANGELS HAVE THE FORM OF MEN OR WOMEN

Inasmuch as angels are the offspring of God, it should be evident that they are in the form of men or women. One Latter-day Saint scholar wrote, "In form angels are like human beings."[8] This agrees with several scriptural passages that identify angels as a man or men. For example, three times the angel who is vital to the story of Manoah and his wife is called "the man" (Judges 13:9–12), the angel Gabriel had "the appearance of a man" (Daniel 8:15), and the angel at Christ's tomb was described as "a young man . . . clothed in a long white garment" (Mark 16:5; see also Luke 24:4).

---

7. *Journal of Discourses*, 16:21. See also Gibbs, Autobiography, in *Writings of Early Latter-day Saints;* I appreciate Matthew B. Brown for sharing this citation with me.
8. Oscar W. McConkie, "Angels," in Ludlow, *Encyclopedia of Mormonism*, 1:40.

ANGELS ARE ORGANIZED INTO CLASSES

The LDS Bible Dictionary states: "These are messengers of the Lord, and are spoken of in the epistle to the Hebrews as 'ministering spirits' (Hebrews 1:14). We learn from latter-day revelation that there are two classes of heavenly beings who minister for the Lord: those who are spirits and those who have bodies of flesh and bone. Spirits are those beings who either have not yet obtained a body of flesh and bone (unembodied), or who have once had a mortal body and have died, and are awaiting the resurrection (disembodied). Ordinarily the word *angel* means those ministering persons who have a body of flesh and bone, being either resurrected from the dead (reembodied), or else translated, as were Enoch, Elijah, etc. (D&C 129)" ("Angels," 608).

LDS scholar Robert L. Millet explained, "An angel may be a resurrected being (D&C 129:1); a translated being; an unembodied spirit, one who has not yet taken a physical body; a disembodied spirit, one who has lived and died and now awaits the resurrection; a mortal who is attentive to the Spirit of God and follows divine direction to assist or bless another; or the Lord himself."[9] Let us briefly examine each of those six categories of angels.

Resurrected beings. Doctrine and Covenants 129:1 refers to "angels, who are resurrected personages, having bodies of flesh and bones." Angels of this category include Peter and James (D&C 27:12–13; 128:20); John the Baptist (D&C 13; Joseph Smith–History 1:68–72); Moses, Elijah, and Elias (D&C 110:11–16); and Moroni, Michael, Gabriel, and Raphael (D&C

---

9. "Angel," in *LDS Beliefs,* 36; see also McConkie, *Angels,* 11–23.

128:20–21). Furthermore, Joseph Smith said of Abel that he "died a righteous man, and therefore has become an angel of God by receiving his body from the dead."[10] Because Jesus Christ was the first person ever resurrected on this sphere, we know that all angelic visitations before the resurrection of Christ were made by either translated beings or spirits.

Translated beings. The prophet Enoch, who is referred to in various passages of scripture (Genesis 5:18–24; Hebrews 11:5; D&C 107:48–57; Moses 6–7), was translated and became a "ministering angel," together with others whom God "held in reserve to be ministering angels unto many planets." Joseph Smith taught that Enoch "is a ministering angel, to minister to those who shall be heirs of salvation, and appeared unto Jude as Abel did unto Paul; therefore Jude spoke of him [Jude 1:14–15]. . . .

"Paul was also acquainted with this character, and received instructions from him. . . .

"Many have supposed that the doctrine of translation was a doctrine whereby men were taken immediately into the presence of God, and into an eternal fulness, but this is a mistaken idea. Their place of habitation is that of the terrestrial order, and a place prepared for such characters He held in reserve to be ministering angels unto many planets, and who as yet have not entered into so great a fulness as those who are resurrected from the dead."[11]

John the Beloved, a translated being, is also a "ministering

---

10. *Teachings of the Prophet Joseph Smith,* 169.
11. *Teachings of the Prophet Joseph Smith,* 170.

angel." The Lord revealed John's translated status: "Yea, he has undertaken a greater work; therefore I will make him as flaming fire and a ministering angel; he shall minister for those who shall be heirs of salvation who dwell on the earth" (D&C 7:6; see also 3 Nephi 28:6–7). Likewise, the Three Nephites, as translated beings, "are as the angels of God" (3 Nephi 28:30). Moses and Elijah, on the Mount of Transfiguration (Matthew 17:1–7), were translated beings.

Unembodied spirits. Unembodied spirits are those that will never receive a body or that have not yet received a body (that is, premortal spirits). Revelation 12 provides examples of unembodied spirits. When John the Revelator wrote of the war in heaven that took place in the premortal sphere, he referred to both Michael's angels (who were also God's angels) and Satan's angels: "And there was war in heaven: Michael and his angels fought against the dragon; and the dragon fought and his angels, and prevailed not; neither was their place found any more in heaven. And the great dragon . . . was cast out into the earth, and his angels were cast out with him" (Revelation 12:7–9).

Another example of an unembodied spirit is recorded in Moses 5, in which an angel converses with Adam (Moses 5:6–7; cf. Moses 5:58). President Joseph Fielding Smith explained, "All angels coming to Adam after the fall were spirits belonging to this earth who had not yet obtained bodies of flesh and bones."[12]

Satan and other devils are unembodied spirits who are also described as angels. Jacob called the devil an angel and those

---

12. *Answers to Gospel Questions,* 2:98.

who become devils "angels to a devil" (2 Nephi 9:8–9; see also 2 Nephi 2:17). Other texts also refer to the devil's angels: "the devil and his angels" (2 Nephi 9:16; cf. Mosiah 26:27; D&C 29:28, 37; 76:33, 36, 44); "angels to the devil" (Jacob 3:11); "the devil laugheth, and his angels rejoice" (3 Nephi 9:2; cf. Moses 7:26); "for if God spared not the angels that sinned" (2 Peter 2:4), and so forth.

Disembodied spirits (spirits of "just men made perfect"; Hebrews 12:22–23). Disembodied spirits are those that have received mortal bodies, have died, and now labor in the spirit world while awaiting resurrection.

The Old Testament refers to angels scores of times. The Hebrew word *malakh,* usually translated "angel," occurs 213 times in the Old Testament. Examples of Old Testament angels from the Lord include the angel who appeared to Hagar (Genesis 16:7–11), the angel who called "out of heaven" to Abraham (Genesis 22:11, 15), Jacob's dream of the ladder with "angels of God ascending and descending on it" (Genesis 28:12), the angel who spoke to Jacob "in a dream" (Genesis 31:11), "the angel of the Lord [who] appeared unto [Moses] in a flame of fire out of the midst of a bush" (Exodus 3:2), the angel who spoke to Elijah (2 Kings 1:2–15), the angel who "smote in the camp of the Assyrians an hundred fourscore and five thousand" (2 Kings 19:35), and many others. As we have said, it is possible that angels before the resurrection of Jesus Christ (who was the first fruits of the grave, or the first to be resurrected) were either spirits (that is, unembodied or disembodied) or translated beings.

Mortals. Some mortals are like angels (for examples, see

Numbers 20:14; 21:21; 22:5). Elder Jeffrey R. Holland spoke of heavenly angels, those beyond the veil, and then he said: "Not all angels are from the other side of the veil. Some of them we walk with and talk with—here, now, every day. Some of them reside in our own neighborhoods. Some of them gave birth to us, and in my case, one of them consented to marry me. Indeed heaven never seems closer than when we see the love of God manifested in the kindness and devotion of people so good and so pure that angelic is the only word that comes to mind."[13]

The Lord. Israel (or Jacob) called God "the Angel which redeemed me from all evil" (Genesis 48:16; see also Exodus 3:2–6; Joshua 5:13–15), and Doctrine and Covenants 133:53 calls Christ "the angel of his presence," who "saved them [the righteous]; and in his love, and in his pity, he redeemed them." Also, just as angels are messengers, so the Lord too is called the "messenger of the covenant" (Malachi 3:1) and the "messenger of salvation" (D&C 93:8).

---

13. "The Ministry of Angels," *Ensign,* Nov. 2008, 30; see also James E. Faust, "How Near to the Angels," *Ensign,* May 1998, 95, 97.

Chapter 2

HOW MANY ANGELS ARE THERE?

[Lehi] saw God sitting upon his throne, surrounded
with numberless concourses of angels.

1 NEPHI 1:8

The scriptures indicate that the Lord has great numbers of angels. Lehi "saw the heavens open, and he thought he saw God sitting upon his throne, surrounded with numberless concourses of angels in the attitude of singing and praising their God" (1 Nephi 1:8). Note that Lehi said "numberless concourses of angels." A *concourse* can mean an assembly or a crowd; and *numberless* means too many to be counted. Lehi, therefore, envisioned innumerable assemblies or groups of angels who were praising God.

Alma stands as another witness to what Lehi saw. In fact, Alma quotes part of Nephi's record of Lehi's vision (1 Nephi 1:8). In Alma 36, Alma recounts his conversion story to his son Helaman and testifies, "Yea, methought I saw, even as our father Lehi saw, God sitting upon his throne, surrounded with numberless concourses of angels, in the attitude of singing and praising their God; yea, and my soul did long to be there" (Alma 36:22).

John the Revelator adds additional evidence regarding the

great number of angels: "And I beheld, and I heard the voice of many angels round about the throne and the beasts and the elders: and the number of them was ten thousand times ten thousand, and thousands of thousands" (Revelation 5:11). John beheld one hundred million (ten thousand times ten thousand equals one hundred million), and "thousands of thousands" of angels near God's throne. The number may be taken literally, but more likely it signifies an indefinite number. In any case, John witnesses an immense number of angels praising the Lamb. Joseph Smith stated that John the Revelator "gazed upon the glories of the eternal world, saw an innumerable company of angels and heard the voice of God."[1]

Two passages of scripture, one ancient and one modern, use the expression "an innumerable company of angels." Paul wrote in his letter to the Hebrews, "But ye are come unto mount Sion, and unto the city of the living God, the heavenly Jerusalem, and to an innumerable company of angels" (Hebrews 12:22). And Doctrine and Covenants 76:67 states, "These are they who have come to an innumerable company of angels, to the general assembly and church of Enoch, and of the Firstborn."

A scriptural text from Jesus Christ's mortal ministry sets forth the great numbers of the Lord's angels. After Jesus left the Garden of Gethsemane, he encountered Judas, who approached with "a great multitude with swords and staves." During this event, "one of them which were with Jesus stretched out his hand, and drew his sword, and struck a servant of the high priest's and smote off

---

1. *History of the Church,* 5:30.

his ear. Then said Jesus unto him, Put up again thy sword into his place. . . . Thinkest thou that I cannot pray to my Father, and he shall presently give me more than twelve legions of angels?" (Matthew 26:47, 51–53). A legion consists of 3,000 to 6,000 persons; twelve legions are 36,000 to 72,000 persons. But like that of John in Revelation, Jesus's expression perhaps denotes a symbolic figure rather than a specific number. Similarly, Elder Erastus Snow employed the expression "twelve legions" when he described the numbers of angels who visited Saints who attended the dedication of the Kirtland Temple.[2]

Other authorities also refer to great numbers of angels. President Heber C. Kimball taught that "the Lord has said that there are more [angels] for us than there can be against us."[3] And finally, Elder John A. Widtsoe wrote of "uncounted" hosts of angels: "An examination of sacred history makes clear that under the most general definition, angels are personages out of the spirit world, sent to earth as messengers of the Lord. This is in full accord with gospel doctrine. The spiritual, invisible world out of which man comes and into which he returns, is filled with uncounted hosts of such personages."[4]

2. "Sketch Book," 6.
3. *Journal of Discourses*, 3:230.
4. *Evidences and Reconciliations*, 107.

Chapter 3

SOME ANGELS WEAR WHITE CLOTHING

*[Moroni] had on a loose robe of most exquisite
whiteness. It was a whiteness beyond anything earthly
I had ever seen . . . exceedingly white and brilliant.*

JOSEPH SMITH–HISTORY 1:31

Joseph Smith once related that "a man came to me in Kirtland, and told me he had seen an angel, and described his dress [clothing]. I told him he had seen no angel, and that there was no dress [of that nature] in heaven."[1] Owing to his considerable experience with angels, the Prophet, of course, knew about their clothing. In fact, dozens of accounts in scripture and elsewhere refer to the form of dress for the Lord's angels. From these various accounts, it is evident that some angels wear white apparel.

On Sunday morning, the day of Jesus Christ's resurrection, a number of mortals witnessed angels keeping watch at Christ's tomb. All four Gospel writers write concerning the angels' white or shining apparel. Matthew writes, "The two angels of the Lord descended from heaven, and came and rolled back the stone from

---

1. *History of the Church,* 5:267.

the door, and sat upon it. And their countenance was like lightning, and their raiment white as snow" (JST, Matthew 28:2–3).
Mark tells of Mary Magdalene, Salome, and Mary the mother of
James visiting the tomb, "And entering into the sepulchre, they
saw a young man sitting on the right side, clothed in a long white
garment" (Mark 16:5). Luke declares that Mary Magdalene,
Joanna, Mary the mother of James, and other women "found the
stone rolled away from the sepulchre. And they entered in, and
found not the body of the Lord Jesus. And it came to pass, as
they were much perplexed thereabout, behold, two men stood by
them in shining garments" (Luke 24:2–4). And John informs us
that Mary Magdalene wept outside of the tomb, and "as she wept,
she stooped down, and looked into the sepulchre, and seeth two
angels in white sitting, the one at the head, and the other at the
feet, where the body of Jesus had lain" (John 20:11–12).

Two angels were present at Jesus's ascension into heaven from
the Mount of Olives when "a cloud received him out" of the view
of the mortals who remained on the mount. These angels were
dressed in "white apparel" (Acts 1:9–10).

Moroni wore brilliant white clothing when he appeared to
the young prophet. Joseph Smith described the angel's clothing:
"He had on a loose robe of most exquisite whiteness. It was a
whiteness beyond anything earthly I had ever seen; nor do I believe that any earthly thing could be made to appear so exceedingly white and brilliant" (Joseph Smith–History 1:31). Another
text, revealed to the Prophet in April 1830, provides additional
details of a holy angel's garments, which "were pure and white
above all other whiteness" (D&C 20:6). Two additional examples

also come from the scriptures. The seven angels who will come out of the temple in heaven "having the seven plagues" will be "clothed in pure and white linen, and having their breasts girded with golden girdles" (Revelation 15:6). In his vision of John the apostle, Nephi stated, "I looked and beheld a man, and he was dressed in a white robe" (1 Nephi 14:19).

Why do angels often wear white? White signifies purity, glory, and power. Brigham Young spoke of the white clothing of angels: "This company before me tonight does not begin to be adorned inside or out as they should be in order to meet with the angels in heaven who are adorned in purity, power, and glory, clothed with clean white linen."[2]

---

2. Woodruff, Journal, Jan. 2, 1854.

Chapter 4

ANGELS ARE PERSONAGES OF LIGHT, GLORY, AND BEAUTY

*[Moroni's] whole person was glorious beyond
description, and his countenance truly like lightning.
The room was exceedingly light, but not so very
bright as immediately around his person.*

JOSEPH SMITH–HISTORY 1:32

God's angels are personages of light, glory, and beauty. The resurrected Moroni is an example of one who shines with great glory. Joseph Smith recorded: "I discovered a light appearing in my room, which continued to increase until the room was lighter than at noonday, when immediately a personage appeared. . . . He had on a loose robe of most exquisite whiteness. It was a whiteness beyond anything earthly I had ever seen; nor do I believe that any earthly thing could be made to appear so exceedingly white and brilliant. . . . Not only was his robe exceedingly white, but his whole person was glorious beyond description, and his countenance truly like lightning. The room was exceedingly light, but not so very bright as immediately around his person" (Joseph Smith–History 1:30–32).

Joseph Smith described the personage of Moroni with such

words as *light, noonday, lightning,* and *bright* (Joseph Smith–History 1:30–32, 43). He used comparisons to describe the brightness: "lighter than at noonday" (v. 30) and "his countenance truly like lightning" (v. 32). He also compared the "heavenly light" (v. 43) with "earthly" light (v. 31). To attempt to describe the brilliance of the light, the Prophet used "exceedingly light" (v. 32) and "very bright" (v. 32).

Oliver Cowdery wrote a letter about Moroni's visit to Joseph. In this letter, which was published in the *Messenger and Advocate,* Oliver described the brilliant light that accompanied the angel's visit: "On a sudden a light like that of day, only of a purer and far more glorious appearance and brightness, burst into the room.— Indeed, to use [Joseph's] own description, the first sight was as though the house was filled with consuming and unquenchable fire. This sudden appearance of a light so bright, as must naturally be expected, occasioned a shock or sensation, visible to the extremities of the body. It was, however, followed with a calmness and serenity of mind, and an overwhelming rapture of joy that surpassed understanding, and in a moment a personage stood before him.

"Notwithstanding the room was previously filled with light above the brightness of the sun, as I have before described, yet there seemed to be an additional glory surrounding or accompanying this personage, which shone with an increased degree of brilliancy, of which he was in the midst; and though his countenance was as lightning, yet it was of a pleasing, innocent and glorious appearance, so much so, that every fear was banished from the heart, and nothing but calmness pervaded the soul."[1]

John the Baptist, like Moroni an angelic minister, was attended with magnificent light and glory when he appeared to Joseph Smith and Oliver Cowdery. Joseph related, "While we were thus employed, praying, and calling upon the Lord, a messenger from heaven, descended in a cloud of light."[2] In April conference of 2007, Elder L. Tom Perry spoke of Oliver Cowdery's description of John's visitation: "'On a sudden, as from the midst of eternity, the voice of the Redeemer spake peace to us, while the vail was parted and the angel of God came down clothed with glory, and delivered the anxiously looked for message, and the keys of the gospel of repentance!—What joy! what wonder! what amazement! . . .' (*Messenger and Advocate*, Oct. 1834, 15)."[3]

Beyond the accounts of the visits of Moroni and John the Baptist are numerous other accounts in both scripture and Church history of the light that may accompany God's angels. Early in the morning on Resurrection Sunday, an angel removed the huge stone that covered the entrance to Jesus's tomb. This angel had a "countenance . . . like lightning": "The angel of the Lord

---

1. "Letter No. 4," *Messenger and Advocate* 1 (Feb. 1835): 79; spelling standardized. David Whitmer, who like Oliver Cowdery was one of the witnesses of the Book of Mormon, described the angel's light: "It was not like the light of the sun nor like that of a fire, but more glorious and beautiful." *Millennial Star* 40 (Dec. 9, 1878): 772; see also Roberts, *Comprehensive History*, 1:143–44.

2. Jessee, *Papers of Joseph Smith*, 1:290; see also *Times and Seasons* 3 (Aug. 1, 1842): 865–66.

3. "The Message of the Restoration," *Ensign*, May 2007, 87.

descended from heaven, and came and rolled back the stone from the door, and sat upon it. His countenance was like lightning, and his raiment white as snow" (Matthew 28:2–3). Doctrine and Covenants 20 similarly describes the countenance of an unnamed angel (perhaps Moroni) that ministered to Joseph Smith: "God ministered unto him by an holy angel, whose countenance was as lightning" (D&C 20:6).

The prophets often used symbolic language to express an angel's light and glory. Ezekiel, for example, wrote of an angel that had an "appearance . . . like the appearance of brass" (Ezekiel 40:3). Ezekiel is employing a figure of speech that describes the messenger's brightness, glory, and beauty—such as polished brass.[4] In a similar way, John described the brilliant light and glory of a "mighty angel" (Revelation 10:1) with four symbolic expressions: *cloud, rainbow, sun,* and *fire:* "And I saw another mighty angel come down from heaven, clothed with a cloud: and a rainbow was upon his head, and his face was as it were the sun, and his feet as pillars of fire" (Revelation 10:1). Two expressions exemplify this angel's radiance and light: "a rainbow was upon his head" and "his face was as it were the sun."

Some accounts mention not the light that belongs to the angel's person but instead the splendid light that accompanies the angel. For example, a light accompanied the angel that appeared to Peter while he was imprisoned in Jerusalem: "And, behold, the angel of the Lord came upon him [Peter], and a light shined in

---

4. Similarly, Daniel used symbolic language to describe the Lord's beauty and glory when he saw the Lord in vision: *fine gold, beryl* (a transparent, colorful mineral), *lightning, lamps of fire,* and *polished brass* (see Daniel 10:5–6).

the prison" (Acts 12:7). Although this account does not specifically identify the light as emanating from the angel's person, it is probable that the light that shined in the prison came from the angel.

Similarly, Joseph Smith recorded that a bright light accompanied the angel that appeared to him, Oliver Cowdery, and David Whitmer. Joseph recorded that he and David "knelt down . . . and had not been many minutes engaged in prayer, when presently [they] beheld a light above [them] in the air, of exceeding brightness; and behold, an angel stood before [them]."[5] And Wilford Woodruff described the three heavenly messengers who appeared to him and George A. Smith while they were in Manchester, England, and evil spirits were accosting them. Elder Woodruff wrote that while he was praying for deliverance from the Lord, "the door opened and three messengers entered, and the room was filled with light equal to the blazing light of the sun at mid-day."[6]

The Lord's angels are truly personages of light and glory; they are also beautiful beings, as President Brigham Young made clear. On April 8, 1868, Brigham spoke of "the excellency of the heavens, and of the beauty which dwells in the society of the Gods." He said, "Were you to see an angel, you would see a beautiful and lovely creature."[7] About four years later, he spoke concerning some of the unbecoming fashions of his day: "There is not

5. *History of the Church*, 1:54.
6. *Deseret Weekly* 53 (Oct. 24, 1896): 577; see also Stuy, *Collected Discourses*, 5:199.
7. *Brigham Young*, 134.

a Latter-day Saint nor a Former-day Saint that ever did, or ever will expect to see any such customs or fashions when they get into heaven. If they were to see an angel, they would see a being beautifully but modestly dressed, white, comely [attractive] and nice to look upon."[8] A year later President Young informed the Saints that if an individual were privileged to see a female angel, "she would be . . . perfectly beautiful."[9]

William W. Phelps also recorded an expression of an angel's beauty. After seeing an angel, Brother Phelps wrote: "I cried with a loud voice, The Lord preserve us for an angel is here! The Lord is with us, for his angel has come!! His appearance and countenance were beautiful; and his robe was white. His skin was a touch nicer than virgin snow, tinged with a crimson glimmer of sun-set."[10]

---

8. *Journal of Discourses*, 15:162.

9. *Journal of Discourses*, 16:21.

10. *Latter Day Saints' Messenger and Advocate* 1 (Feb. 1835): 66. For other accounts that describe the beauty of angels, see Gibbs, Autobiography, in *Writings of Early Latter-day Saints*, and John Nicholson, "Temple Manifestations," *Contributor* 16 (1894–95): 117–18.

Chapter 5

HIERARCHY AMONG THE ANGELS

*There are angels of
various appointments and stations.*

PRESIDENT CHARLES W. PENROSE

A hierarchy, or ranking, of authority exists among the Lord's angels. John Taylor referred to "the different grades of angels."[1] "There are angels of various appointments and stations," taught President Charles W. Penrose. "Michael is called an 'archangel.' (D&C 29:26; Daniel 10:13.)."[2] He also stated, "Angels . . . are agents of Deity of different degrees of intelligence, power and authority, under the direction of higher dignitaries, and subject to law and order in their respective spheres."[3]

The following statements demonstrate that there is a hierarchy, or ranking, of the Lord's angels:

1. God the Father, Jesus Christ, and the Holy Ghost are, of course, greater than angels. The Prophet Joseph Smith taught:

"Who and What Are the Angels?" 950.

1. *Gospel Kingdom*, 31.
2. "Who and What Are the Angels?" *Improvement Era* 15 (Aug. 1912): 950.
3. Penrose, "Angels," 950.

"Gods have an ascendency over the angels, who are ministering servants. In the resurrection, some are raised to be angels, others are raised to become Gods."[4] The Prophet also taught: "Then shall they be gods, because they have no end; therefore shall they be from everlasting to everlasting, because they continue; then shall they be above all, because all things are subject unto them. Then shall they be gods, because they have all power, and the angels are subject unto them" (D&C 132:20). The statement that "the angels are subject unto them" accords with a statement in Moroni 7:30, in which Moroni recorded the words of his father, Mormon, that "they [the angels] are subject unto" the Lord. Paul also declared that Jesus Christ was "so much better than the angels" (Hebrews 1:4).

Elder Orson Pratt further clarified: "Some angels are Gods, and still possess the lower office called angels. Adam is called an Archangel, yet he is a God. Abraham, Isaac and Jacob, no doubt, have the right to officiate in the capacity of angels if they choose, but still they have ascended to their exaltation, to a higher state than that of angels—namely, to thrones, kingdoms, principalities and powers, to reign over kingdoms and to hold the everlasting Priesthood."[5]

2. Of all the angels—resurrected beings, translated beings, or spirits—Michael (Adam) is the head angel; the scriptures call him the *archangel* (1 Thessalonians 4:16; Jude 1:9; D&C 29:26; 88:112; 107:54; 128:21). The term *arch*—part of such words as

---

4. *Teachings of the Prophet Joseph Smith*, 312.
5. *Journal of Discourses*, 8:187.

patri*arch, arch*etype, *arch*bishop, *arch*enemy, *arch*conservative, and *arch*scoundrel—means "chief, principal, or preeminent." Michael, then, is the chief of angels; Joseph Smith explained that Michael stands next in authority to Jesus Christ himself "and presides over the spirits of all men."[6]

3. The angel Gabriel, who is Noah, is next in authority after Michael. Joseph Smith taught: "The Priesthood was first given to Adam; he obtained the First Presidency. . . . He is Michael the Archangel, spoken of in the Scriptures. Then to Noah, who is Gabriel: he stands next in authority to Adam in the Priesthood."[7]

4. Is Raphael next in authority after Gabriel? We do not know who stands in authority after Gabriel, although it may be Raphael. Doctrine and Covenants 128:21 refers to Michael (the chief angel), then Gabriel (second in authority), then Raphael (possibly third, but not specified), then "divers angels": "And the voice of Michael, the archangel; the voice of Gabriel, and of Raphael, and of divers angels . . ." (D&C 128:21). Could this listing of angels be presented in the sequence of their authority—Michael, Gabriel, Raphael, and then various angels? We currently have no authoritative answer to this question.

5. Angels who have bodies of flesh and bone, meaning those angels who are either translated or resurrected, have greater power than beings who are spirits. Joseph Smith explained: "All beings who have bodies have power over those who have not. The devil has no power over us only as we permit him."[8] The Prophet also

---

6. *Teachings of the Prophet Joseph Smith,* 157.
7. *Teachings of the Prophet Joseph Smith,* 157.
8. Ehat and Cook, *Words of Joseph Smith,* 60.

taught: "There are three independent principles—the spirit of God, the spirit of man, and the spirit of the devil. All men have power to resist the devil. They who have tabernacles have power over those who have not."[9]

6. John "saw a strong angel proclaiming with a loud voice" (Revelation 5:2). The identity of the "strong angel" is not revealed. It may be Michael, Gabriel, Raphael, or any other mighty angel. Not all angels are described as strong. We do not know where this "strong angel" is in the hierarchy.

7. Revelation 10:1–3 describes another powerful angel: "And I saw another mighty angel come down from heaven, clothed with a cloud: and a rainbow was upon his head, and his face was as it were the sun, and his feet as pillars of fire: And he had in his hand a little book open: and he set his right foot upon the sea, and his left foot on the earth, and he cried with a loud voice, as when a lion roareth." This angel possesses great power; only three times in Revelation are the angels called "mighty" (Revelation 5:2; 10:1; 18:21; see also Daniel 4:13). Beyond the adjective *mighty* that describes the angel, several symbolic expressions serve to demonstrate the greatness of this angel: "come down from heaven," "clothed with a cloud," "a rainbow was upon his head," "his face was as it were the sun," "his feet as pillars of fire," "he set his right foot upon the sea, and his left foot on the earth," and "he cried with a loud voice, as when a lion roareth." We do not know the hierarchal status of this angel, but John's description of him indicates that he possesses great power.

---

9. Ehat and Cook, *Words of Joseph Smith*, 74.

Chapter 6

ANGELS' EXTRAORDINARY CAPABILITIES AND POWERS

※⁂※ ⁂※

*[Moroni] appeared at my bedside, standing in
the air, for his feet did not touch the floor.*

Joseph Smith—History 1:30

In October 1998, President Gordon B. Hinckley stated in general conference, "I think about the power and force of angels that stand among us."[1] Indeed, scriptural texts indicate that the Lord's angels have extraordinary capabilities and powers, making them formidable beings. Angels may have power over the elements, and the various earthly forces that exist in this telestial world do not bind them. These great powers of angels enable them to fulfill their missions here upon the earth and to assist mortals, who are, in comparison, delicate and frail. As we discuss the extraordinary powers of angels, however, we must remain cautious and open about those powers, because there is so much that we do not know. We must also remember that many scriptural statements, especially those from John the Revelator, contain symbolisms.

---

1. "To the Boys and to the Men," *Ensign*, Nov. 1998, 52.

The miraculous powers of angels build confidence among mortals who understand angelic authority and powers. Not all angels, of course, have equal power and authority: Angels with resurrected bodies have greater power than do translated beings, which in turn have greater power than do angels who are either unembodied or disembodied spirits. Depending on their rank and status and the errand on which they are sent, angels may have some or all of the following powers:

- Power over gravity
- Power over the elements
- Other superhuman powers and capabilities, including the power to appear seemingly out of nowhere and vanish in an instant; to cause doors to open of their own accord; to cause chains to fall from bound prisoners; to mingle undetected with mortals; to pass through walls, closed doors, and ceilings; to escape earth's pits and depths; to remain unharmed in fiery furnaces and among wild beasts

Angels have power over gravity

Heavenly beings have no need to stand on the ground or the floor. They may stand above the ground or floor, perhaps to remain elevated above telestial creatures, or perhaps the place where humans stand is considered profane space. In several instances, the Lord, while visiting his prophets, stood on a paved work of precious materials, such as gold (D&C 110:2) or sapphire stone (Exodus 24:10). Joseph Smith testified that "when the light rested upon me I saw two Personages, whose brightness and glory defy all description, standing above me in the air" (Joseph Smith–History 1:17).

President Lorenzo Snow saw the resurrected Lord in the Salt Lake Temple standing "about three feet above the floor" and remarked that "it looked as though he stood on a plate of solid gold."[2] Elder George F. Richards had an inspired vision of Jesus Christ during which, he stated, "I was in the presence of my Savior as he stood in mid-air."[3]

There are also recorded instances of angels standing in the air. Moroni's feet did not touch the floor during his visits to Joseph Smith on September 21, 1823. While the young prophet was praying, Moroni "appeared at [his] bedside, standing in the air, for his feet did not touch the floor" (Joseph Smith–History 1:30). In addition to his ability to stand in the air, note Moroni's power to ascend to heaven: "After [Moroni's] communication, I [Joseph Smith] . . . saw, as it were, a conduit open right up into heaven, and he ascended till he entirely disappeared" (Joseph Smith–History 1:43). Oliver Cowdery testified before a court that he saw a "glorious messenger from heaven, dressed in white, standing above the ground, in a glory I have never seen anything compare with, the sun insignificant in comparison."[4]

---

2. *Deseret News*, Apr. 2, 1938.

3. Kimball, "The Cause Is Just and Worthy," *Ensign*, May 1974, 119.

4. Nibley, *Missionary Experiences*, 296. Other accounts of angels standing in the air include, for example, the accounts of Wilford Woodruff (Journal, Nov. 8, 1857) and Benjamin Brown, a contemporary of Joseph Smith (Harper, "'Pentecost and Endowment Indeed,'" in Welch and Carlson, *Opening the Heavens*, 336).

These accounts demonstrate that heavenly beings have the power to stand, apparently unsupported, in the air; additionally, several scriptural passages relate that angels descended from heaven, thus providing additional evidence that they have power over gravity. For example, the angel who appeared to Alma and the sons of Mosiah "descended as it were in a cloud" (Mosiah 27:11), and Nephi and Lehi and about three hundred persons witnessed "the heavens open; and angels came down out of heaven and ministered unto them" (Helaman 5:48). The multitude of Saints who were with the resurrected Jesus "saw the heavens open, and they saw angels descending out of heaven as it were in the midst of fire" (3 Nephi 17:24). Further, the phrase "angels came down out of heaven" is found, with minor variations, in such other scriptural passages as "angels did come down out of heaven" (3 Nephi 19:14) and "[John] saw another mighty angel come down from heaven" (Revelation 10:1; see also 18:1; 20:1).

Angels have power over the elements

With regard to angels' knowledge of the elements and the "laws of nature," Elder John A. Widtsoe explained that angels are "vivid personages, intelligent beings vastly superior to man, knowing well the laws of nature and therefore able to control them."[5] While president of the Church, Brigham Young made statements regarding the power that angels have over the

---

5. *Rational Theology*, 72.

elements.[6] Other Church leaders, too, have taught about angels' power over the elements.[7]

Using symbolic language, John the Revelator writes of angels who have many great powers: One angel has "power over fire" (Revelation 14:18), four angels have power over "the four winds of the earth" (Revelation 7:1), and one or more angels have power over the fate of the waters; note that John refers specifically to "the angel of the waters" (Revelation 16:5; see vv. 3–5, 12).

Furthermore, there are four angels in Revelation, "to whom is given power over the four parts of the earth, to save life and to destroy; . . . having power to shut up the heavens, to seal up unto life, or to cast down to the regions of darkness" (D&C 77:8; see also Revelation 7:1). Again, using symbolic language, John the Revelator states that "a mighty angel took up a stone like a great millstone, and cast it into the sea, saying, Thus with violence shall that great city Babylon be thrown down, and shall be found no more at all" (Revelation 18:21; cf. Jer. 51:60–64). This action by an angel symbolizes the destruction of wickedness in the last days. Although this angel is unnamed, the fact that he is *mighty* is significant, as is the idea that God will empower one of his angels to destroy Babylon.

Angels who have power over fire (again, watch for the symbolism) include the angel spoken of in Exodus 3, which records

6. See, for example, *Journal of Discourses*, 15:127; 16:113; 19:36–37.

7. See, for example, Taylor, *Gospel Kingdom*, 31; Kimball, *Journal of Discourses*, 4:2; Hyde, *Journal of Discourses*, 6:368; and George Q. Cannon, "A Dream," *Juvenile Instructor* 32, no. 21 (Nov. 1, 1897): 656.

that Moses encountered an angel appearing "in a flame of fire": "And the angel of the Lord appeared unto him in a flame of fire out of the midst of a bush: and he looked, and, behold, the bush burned with fire, and the bush was not consumed" (Exodus 3:2). This must have been an astonishing scene for this man who was tending flocks in the desert. The account of the angel appearing in a flame of fire was of such significance that Stephen, more than a millennium later, twice referred to it in his speech to the Sanhedrin (Acts 7:30, 35). In sum, the angel's appearance in fire signifies a great miracle.

Angels have demonstrated power over fire on several other occasions: "For it came to pass, when the flame went up toward heaven from off the altar, that the angel of the Lord ascended in the flame of the altar. And Manoah and his wife looked on it, and fell on their faces to the ground" (Judges 13:20). Also, the Book of Mormon records that a multitude "saw angels descending out of heaven as it were in the midst of fire" (3 Nephi 17:24).

Angels have many other superhuman powers and capabilities

In addition to having power over gravity and the elements, angels possess many other extraordinary abilities. For example, angels can appear seemingly out of nowhere and then vanish (see chapter 7). They can appear to mortals and hide their angelic nature, and they have the ability to appear as mortals (see chapter 8).

The angel who saved Peter the night before he was to be executed possessed great powers. This angel miraculously entered the prison and caused Peter's chains to fall "from his hands" (Acts

12:7; cf. Abraham 1:15, which records that an angel unloosed Abraham's bands). Then the angel and Peter walked unseen "past the first and the second ward," presumably where guards were stationed: another miracle by the angel (Acts 12:10). When Peter and the angel approached the "iron gate that leadeth unto the city," it opened by itself; or, rather, it opened because of the angel's powers. The angel demonstrated four powers: (1) He was able to miraculously enter into a prison, although it had locked gates or doors and several guards; (2) he caused the chains that bound Peter's hands to fall off; (3) he and Peter walked undetected past two sets of guards ("the first and the second ward"); and (4) the angel caused the outer iron gate, which presumably was locked, to open.

Chains binding prisoners are no obstacle to angels. Elder Parley P. Pratt, after spending several months in a Missouri dungeon, was freed by an angel. Neither the walls and the doors nor the chains that bound Elder Pratt could prevent the angel's freeing him. "On the grand national Anniversary of American independence, the glorious 4th of July, [Parley] being instructed and warned, by an Angel of the Lord, in a vision of the night, burst his chains, threw open his prison doors, and emerged forth from his prison: and after wandering for near a week, night and day, almost without food, he avoided all pursuit and arrived at the residence of his family."[8]

Yet another account pertains to the great power of angels. When he was called to deliver the Israelites from their foes,

8. "Biography of Nathan Pratt," *Times and Seasons* 5 (Jan. 15, 1844): 414.

Gideon expressed his feelings of inadequacy: "Oh my Lord, wherewith shall I save Israel? behold, my family is poor in Manasseh, and I am the least in my father's house" (Judges 6:15). The Lord responded by promising, "Surely I will be with thee, and thou shalt smite the Midianites as one man" (Judges 6:16). Then to give Gideon confidence that the Lord would fulfill his word, God's angel performed a great miracle: "And the angel of God said unto him, Take the flesh and the unleavened cakes, and lay them upon this rock, and pour out the broth. And he did so. Then the angel of the Lord put forth the end of the staff that was in his hand, and touched the flesh and the unleavened cakes; and there rose up fire out of the rock, and consumed the flesh and the unleavened cakes. Then the angel of the Lord departed out of his sight" (Judges 6:20–21). After these events, the Lord empowered Gideon to defeat the Midianites (Judges 7:2–8:21). Gideon became so great in the eyes of the Israelites that they invited him to become king, but he refused (Judges 8:22–23).

Sometimes the astounding power of angels causes the earth to quake. For instance, on the day of Jesus Christ's resurrection, the descent of an angel caused the earth to shake: "And, behold, there was a great earthquake: for the angel of the Lord descended from heaven" (Matthew 28:2). Also, "the angel of the Lord appeared . . . and he descended as it were in a cloud; and he spake as it were with a voice of thunder, which caused the earth to shake upon which they stood" (Mosiah 27:11). And "with their own eyes they had beheld an angel of the Lord; and his voice was as thunder, which shook the earth; and they knew that there was nothing save the power of God that could shake the earth and cause it to tremble as though it would part asunder" (Mosiah 27:18). And also, "I have seen an angel face to face, and he spake with me, and his voice was as thunder, and it shook the whole earth" (Alma 38:7).

THE THREE NEPHITES: EXTRAORDINARY CAPABILITIES AND POWERS

Jesus promised the Three Nephites extraordinary powers: "For ye shall never taste of death. . . . And ye shall never endure the pains of death. . . . And again, ye shall not have pain while ye shall dwell in the flesh, neither sorrow save it be for the sins of the world" (3 Nephi 28:7–9). The phrases "ye shall never taste of death" and "ye shall never endure the pains of death" specify that they will never die because of diseases, illnesses, plagues, pestilence, accidents, weapons, calamities or disasters, natural causes, aging, or a thousand other things that mortals die of. The phrase "ye shall not have pain while ye shall dwell in the flesh" indicates that they will not suffer from such painful human conditions as injuries, sicknesses, diseases, aches, sores, wounds, cuts, broken bones, and more. As Joseph Smith explained, "Translation obtains deliverance from the tortures and sufferings of the body, but their existence will prolong as to the labors and toils of the ministry, before they can enter into so great a rest and glory."[9]

Mormon explained the change in the Three Nephites' mortal condition so that they would "not taste of death": "I have inquired of the Lord, and he hath made it manifest unto me . . . that they might not taste of death there was a change wrought

---

9. *Teachings of the Prophet Joseph Smith,* 171.

upon their bodies, that they might not suffer pain nor sorrow save it were for the sins of the world. Now this change was not equal to that which shall take place at the last day; but there was a change wrought upon them, insomuch that Satan could have no power over them, that he could not tempt them; and they were sanctified in the flesh, that they were holy, and that the powers of the earth could not hold them" (3 Nephi 28:37–39).

Mormon described additional powers of the Three Nephites: "They were cast into prison by them who did not belong to the church. And the prisons could not hold them, for they were rent in twain. And they were cast down into the earth; but they did smite the earth with the word of God, insomuch that by his power they were delivered out of the depths of the earth; and therefore they could not dig pits sufficient to hold them. And thrice they were cast into a furnace and received no harm. And twice were they cast into a den of wild beasts; and behold they did play with the beasts as a child with a suckling lamb, and re-ceived no harm" (3 Nephi 28:19–22).

In sum, the Three Nephites demonstrated authority over earthly powers and elements: Prison walls could not hold them, earth's pits and depths were no threat to them, fiery furnaces had no power to destroy them, and even wild beasts could not harm them.

Chapter 7

ANGELS MAY BE "SEEN OR UNSEEN"

❦

Usually [angels] are not *seen. Sometimes they are.*
But seen or unseen they are always *near.*

ELDER JEFFREY R. HOLLAND

In the 2008 October general conference, Elder Jeffrey R. Holland gave a landmark address on the ministry of angels. He declared: "I testify of angels, both the heavenly and the mortal kind. In doing so I am testifying that God never leaves us alone, never leaves us unaided in the challenges that we face." Then Elder Holland explained: "On occasions, global or personal, we may feel we are distanced from God, shut out from heaven, lost, alone in dark and dreary places. Often enough that distress can be of our own making, but even then the Father of us all is watching and assisting. And always there are those angels who come and go all around us, seen and unseen, known and unknown, mortal and immortal."[1]

Angels' operations and ministrations are largely unknown

"The Ministry of Angels," *Ensign*, Nov. 2008, 29.

1. "Ministry of Angels," 31.

to human beings. Angels can move about the earth conducting the Lord's divine work, and they may serve, minister, and mingle among mortals without the awareness of mortals. Elder Parley P. Pratt's words are instructive: Angels "can also be present without being visible to mortals."[2] Elder John A. Widtsoe taught: "These vivid personages, intelligent beings vastly superior to man, . . . may visit with man, though not seen with the natural eye. Most probably we walk among a company of such invisible, intelligent spirits."[3]

The Three Nephites can appear undetected to mortals. Mormon wrote of them: "Behold they will be among the Gentiles, and the Gentiles shall know them not. They will also be among the Jews, and the Jews shall know them not. . . . And they are as the angels of God, and if they shall pray unto the Father in the name of Jesus they can show themselves unto whatsoever man it seemeth them good" (3 Nephi 28:27–28, 30).

The following accounts of two visions, both from Joseph Smith's writings, are examples of heavenly beings ministering among mortals undetected. Regarding the first, dated January 1836, Joseph Smith recorded that he had a vision of Brigham Young preaching the gospel to several hostile men. But an angel of God, with a drawn sword in his hand, provided protection to Brigham, although Brigham was unable to detect his presence.[4] The second vision pertains to an undetected visitation by Jesus Christ. The Prophet related: "I saw the 12 apostles of the Lamb,

2. *Key to the Science of Theology,* 113.
3. *Rational Theology,* 72.
4. See *History of the Church,* 2:381.

who are now upon the earth, who hold the keys of this last ministry, in foreign lands, standing together in a circle, much fatigued, with their clothes tattered and feet swollen, with their eyes cast downward, and Jesus (standing) in their midst, and they did not behold him; the Savior looked upon them and wept."[5]

A narrative from the book of Numbers exemplifies the concept that angels can minister undetected among mortals. Balaam had multiple interactions with Balak, the king of Moab. On one occasion, Balaam journeyed with the king's officers. The text states that "Balaam rose up in the morning, and saddled his ass, and went with the princes of Moab. And God's anger was kindled because he went: and the angel of the Lord stood in the way for an adversary against him. Now he was riding upon his ass, and his two servants were with him. And the ass saw the angel of the Lord standing in the way, and his sword drawn in his hand: and the ass turned aside out of the way, and went into the field: and Balaam smote the ass, to turn her into the way" (Numbers 22:21–23). As the narrative points out, the donkey saw the angel standing in the path with a sword in his hand, but Balaam did not. Likely thinking his animal was just being stubborn, Balaam hit it to encourage it to move forward on the path.

The narrative describes the presence of the angel and the persistent tension between Balaam and his animal: "But the angel of the Lord stood in a path of the vineyards, a wall being on this side, and a wall on that side. And when the ass saw the angel of the Lord, she thrust herself unto the wall, and crushed Balaam's foot

---

5. Jessee, *Papers of Joseph Smith*, 2:157.

against the wall: and he smote her again. And the angel of the Lord went further, and stood in a narrow place, where was no way to turn either to the right hand or to the left. And when the ass saw the angel of the Lord, she fell down under Balaam: and Balaam's anger was kindled, and he smote the ass with a staff" (Numbers 22:24–27). Three times Balaam, in great anger, smote the beast with a staff. In fact, in his anger, Balaam declared that he would have killed the beast with a sword had he possessed one (see v. 29).

In due course, the Lord enabled Balaam to see the angel. "Then the Lord opened the eyes of Balaam, and he saw the angel of the Lord standing in the way, and his sword drawn in his hand: and he bowed down his head, and fell flat on his face" (Numbers 22:31).

This unique narrative provides several details about angels: (1) angels may possess swords; (2) the donkey of this story was permitted to see the angel with the sword and also to converse with Balaam; (3) angels may minister among mortals undetected; and (4) angels may also make themselves known to mortals according to the power and desire of heavenly authorities.

Speaking at Brother Charles Little's funeral, Brigham Young taught that spirits can minister to mortals without detection: "Spirits administer to us but we do not know it. Charles Little here, will administer to his mother, but she will not know it. . . . The living cannot see the departed spirits, but the latter can see and administer to those in the flesh, even though the latter know it not."[6]

---

6. Cowley, *Wilford Woodruff*, 415–16.

Elder Orson Hyde delivered a speech on July 4, 1854, in
the Tabernacle in Salt Lake City on patriotism, liberty, and the
Declaration of Independence. During his speech, Elder Hyde
spoke of an angel who worked behind the scenes with Columbus,
during the American Revolution, and at other times in American
history. "This same angel presides over the destinies of America,
and feels a lively interest in all our doings. He was in the camp
of Washington; and, *by an invisible hand,* led on our fathers to
conquest and victory; and all this to open and prepare the way
for the Church and kingdom of God to be established on the
western hemisphere, for the redemption of Israel and the salvation of the world. This same angel was with Columbus, and gave
him deep impressions, by dreams and by visions, respecting this
New World. Trammeled by poverty and by an unpopular cause,
yet his persevering and unyielding heart would not allow an obstacle in his way too great for him to overcome; and the angel
of God helped him—was with him on the stormy deep, calmed
the troubled elements, and guided his frail vessel to the desired
haven. Under the guardianship of this same angel, or Prince of
America, have the United States grown, increased, and flourished,
like the sturdy oak by the rivers of water."[7]

7. *Journal of Discourses,* 6:368; italics added.

Chapter 8

ANGELS MAY
APPEAR AS MORTALS

❧❧❧ ❀❀❀

Be not forgetful to entertain strangers: for thereby
some have entertained angels unawares.

HEBREWS 13:2

Angels who are resurrected or translated are able to conceal their angelic characteristics, including their great light and glory, and mingle among human beings as if they were mortals. When writing his epistle to the Hebrews, the apostle Paul taught an important truth: "Be not forgetful to entertain strangers: for thereby some have entertained angels unawares" (Hebrews 13:2). As this verse suggests, mortals have hosted or seen angels without knowing that they were hosting such messengers. Joseph Smith provided additional knowledge on this matter: "The spirit of a just man made perfect, if he made his appearance he would appear or be enveloped in flaming fire, and no man in this mortal state could endure it, but an angel could come and appear as another man, for Paul says, 'be careful to entertain strangers, for some have entertained angels unawares' [Hebrews 13:2]."[1]

---

1. Ehat and Cook, *Words of Joseph Smith*, 255.

ANGELS

The story of the resurrected Lord appearing to Cleopas and another man on the road to Emmaus illustrates how celestial beings can conceal their glory and appear as mere mortals (see Luke 24). The occasion was Resurrection Sunday. The Lord had risen earlier that day, and the tomb was empty. The text explains: "And behold, two of them went that same day to a village called Emmaus, which was from Jerusalem about threescore furlongs. And they talked together of all these things which had happened. And it came to pass, that, while they communed together and reasoned, Jesus himself drew near, and went with them. But their eyes were holden that they should not know him" (Luke 24:13–16). The expression "their eyes were holden" indicates that these two men were unable to recognize the celestial nature of Jesus Christ as he walked beside them.

A question asked by one of the men further indicates that their eyes were restrained: "Art thou only a stranger in Jerusalem, and hast thou not known the things which are come to pass there in these days?" This man would not have been asked this question if the two men had comprehended Jesus's celestial nature. The omniscient Jesus played the role of a mortal by responding, "What things?" (Luke 24:19). The conversation continues for an unspecified time. Once the two men arrived at their village, "they constrained [Jesus], saying, Abide with us: for it is toward evening, and the day is far spent. And he went in to tarry with them" (Luke 24:29). Jesus broke and blessed bread and gave it to the two men. At this time they were permitted to recognize that this "stranger" was none other than Jesus Christ, their God and their

48

Savior—"And their eyes were opened, and they knew him; and he vanished out of their sight" (Luke 24:31).

The Three Nephites are another example of angels who can hide their angelic characteristics in order to appear as mortals. As translated beings, they possess terrestrial bodies,[2] which enable them to hide their glory when they wish to appear as mortals. The Three Nephites sometimes minister among mortals without revealing their identities (see 3 Nephi 28:27–28).

Mormon testified that he had seen the Three Nephites: "But behold, I have seen them, and they have ministered unto me" (3 Nephi 28:26). Whenever they wish to reveal themselves to mortals, they pray to Heavenly Father in Jesus Christ's name, and then they are permitted to reveal themselves according to what is appropriate and right (see 3 Nephi 28:30).

A story about Joseph Smith and his bodyguard Allen Stout provides yet another example of an encounter with a translated person who concealed his angelic status while fulfilling his mission upon the earth. As Joseph Smith and Allen Stout were walking on a road west of the Mississippi River, "they saw a man walking along a road leading in from the south and coming towards them. The Prophet told Allen to remain where he was while he stepped over to speak with this pedestrian. Allen turned his back towards them and for a time forgot the Prophet and became engaged with his own thoughts, while he stood whipping a low bush with the cane he carried.

"The hand of the Prophet upon his shoulder aroused him.

---

2. See *Teachings of the Prophet Joseph Smith*, 170.

The Prophet said, 'We must return immediately to Nauvoo.' They walked silently and rapidly. Allen became very sorrowful over his recreancy to his duty and could not refrain from weeping. The Prophet asked him why he wept. Allen confessed, 'I am an insufficient bodyguard—criminally neglectful of your welfare. I allowed that man you met to speak with you without even being ready to defend if he attacked you. He could have killed you and made his escape without my knowing who he is, which way he went or what he even looks like. You will have to dispense with my services and take a guard on which you can depend. Your life is too precious to be trusted to my care.'

"The Prophet then said, 'That man would not harm me. You saw John the Revelator.'"[3]

Another account, related by David Whitmer, one of the Three Witnesses of the Book of Mormon, likewise demonstrates that translated or resurrected beings can hide the fact that they are angels: "When I was returning to Fayette with Joseph and Oliver, all of us riding in the wagon, Oliver and I on an old fashioned wooden spring seat and Joseph behind us, we were suddenly approached by a very pleasant, nice looking old man in a clear open place, who saluted us with 'Good morning, it is very warm,' at the same instant wiping his face or forehead with his hand. We returned the salutation and by a sign from Joseph I invited him to ride if he was going our way, but he said very pleasantly, 'No, I am going to Cumorah.' This was something new to me, I did not know what Cumorah meant, and as I looked enquiringly at

---

3. McConkie, *Remembering Joseph*, 210–11.

Joseph, the old man instantly disappeared so that I did not see him again.

" . . . He was, I should think, about 5 feet 9 or 10 inches and heavy set. . . . He was dressed in a suit of brown, woolen clothes; his hair and beard were white. . . . I also remember that he had a sort of knapsack on his back, and something was in it which was shaped like a book. It was the messenger who had the plates."[4]

During the period of the judges in the Old Testament, the Midianites, Amalekites, and other foes of the Israelites conquered Israel and destroyed its crops, food supplies, sheep, oxen, and donkeys. These enemies of Israel were great in number: "They came as grasshoppers for multitude; for both they and their camels were without number: and they entered into the land to destroy it" (Judges 6:5). This devastation was immense, to the point that "Israel was greatly impoverished because of the Midianites; and the children of Israel cried unto the Lord" (Judges 6:6). The Lord responded to Israel's cries and prayers by sending an angel, who called Gideon to leadership and subsequently helped him to defeat Israel's enemies.

When the angel appeared to Gideon, the angel "sat under an oak" near the place in which Gideon was threshing wheat (Judges 6:11). Of all the extant revealed narratives of angels, this is the only account in which the angel sits under a tree. Is the angel posing as a mortal by relaxing under the tree or enjoying the shade? In any case, Gideon does not realize that this angel is a

---

4. Baugh, "Parting the Veil," in Welch and Carlson, *Opening the Heavens,* 269–70; see also Jenson, *Latter-day Saint Biographical Encyclopedia,* 1:267; Whitmer, "Old Man Instantly Disappeared," in *Best-Loved Stories,* 38–39.

heavenly messenger. After Gideon conversed with the angel for a time, Gideon finally "perceived that he was an angel of the Lord." Gideon cried out, "Alas, O Lord God! for because I have seen an angel of the Lord face to face. And the Lord said unto him, Peace be unto thee; fear not: thou shalt not die" (Judges 6:22–23).

Brigham Young summarized the power of angels to appear as mortals: "Should an angel come and converse with any man in the congregation, no other one might know it. He would think the person spoke to him as one speaks to another face to face, when he would not be seen at all, only by the Spirit of God or by vision."[5]

---

5. Woodruff, Journal, June 22, 1851.

Chapter 9

ANGELS MAY APPEAR
AND THEN VANISH

*And their eyes were opened, and they knew
[Jesus]; and he vanished out of their sight.*

LUKE 24:31

A ngels do not necessarily approach mortals in the same way
that other mortals do—walking, entering through doors,
making sounds with each step. Rather, some angelic beings are
able to make their approach in an instant; they have the power
to appear out of nowhere and also to vanish from sight. Luke
24 presents an example of a resurrected personage who vanished
from the sight of mortals. After Jesus broke and blessed bread
and gave it to the two men, they were permitted to recognize that
this "stranger" was none other than Jesus Christ, their God and
Savior: "And their eyes were opened, and they knew him; and
he vanished out of their sight" (Luke 24:31). The text is clear—
Jesus "vanished," or disappeared suddenly, from the sight of these
disciples.

The angel Moroni also appeared, seemingly out of nowhere,
and then departed in an instant. In Joseph Smith–History 1:30,
43–44, the Prophet used the words *immediately, instantly,* and

in an instant to describe the angel's appearance at his bedside. "*Immediately* a personage appeared at my bedside, standing in the air, for his feet did not touch the floor" (italics added). And then Moroni disappeared: "*Instantly* I saw, as it were, a conduit open right up into heaven, and he ascended till he entirely disappeared, and the room was left as it had been before this heavenly light had made its appearance" (italics added). And as Joseph was pondering and marveling on the appearance of an angel, the room began to fill with light again "and *in an instant,* as it were, the same heavenly messenger was again by my bedside" (italics added).

Many accounts from Church history in the latter days pertain to heavenly messengers who disappear from the sight of mortals. Two involving Mary M. Whitmer, the wife of Peter Whitmer Sr. and the mother of five of the Book of Mormon witnesses, record that an angel of God appeared to her and showed her the gold plates. In both of these accounts, we are told that the angel vanished from Mary's presence.

In the first of these two accounts, John C. Whitmer, Mary's grandson, recalled the story this way: "One evening, when (after having done her usual day's work in the house) she went to the barn to milk the cows, she met a stranger carrying something on his back that looked like a knapsack. At first she was a little afraid of him, but when he spoke to her in a kind, friendly tone and began to explain to her the nature of the work which was going on in her house, she was filled with inexpressible joy and satisfaction. He then untied his knapsack and showed her a bundle of plates, which in size and appearance, corresponded with the description subsequently given by the witnesses to the Book of Mormon. This strange person turned the leaves of the book of plates over, leaf after leaf, and also showed her the engravings upon them; after which he told her to be patient and faithful in bearing her burden a little longer, promising that if she would do so, she should be blessed; and her reward would be sure, if she proved faithful to the end. The personage then suddenly vanished with the plates, and where he went, she could not tell."[1]

In the second account involving Mary Whitmer, her grandson John reported the same story and added that the angel who appeared to his grandmother was none other than Moroni: "My grandmother told me that the strange visitor met her as she was going to milk the cows. At first she was afraid of him, but he spoke so kindly to her, explaining to her the nature of the work of translation to go on in her house, that she felt a thrill of inexpressible joy, which removed all fear from her. Comforting words were spoken promising her strength and pleasure in her increased labors, and salvation at the end. Moroni took from his knapsack the plates and exhibited them. . . . The personage then suddenly vanished with the plates, and where he went, she could not tell."[2] On another occasion, David Whitmer, one of the Three Witnesses of the Book of Mormon, traveled with Joseph Smith and Oliver Cowdery from Harmony, Pennsylvania, to Fayette,

---

1. Jenson, *Latter-day Saints Biographical Encyclopedia,* 1:283; see also the account of Mary's son David Whitmer, *Deseret News,* Nov. 16, 1878; and Anderson, *Witnesses,* 30.
2. Edward Stevenson, "The Thirteenth Witness to the Plates of the Book of Mormon," *Millennial Star* 55 (1893): 215.

New York. During this journey they saw Moroni walking along the road (see chapter 8). David invited him to ride with them in the wagon, but Moroni responded, "'No, I am going over to Cumorah,' and suddenly disappeared in the midst of a plain."[3]

---

3. Stevenson, "Thirteenth Witness," 215; see also reports of Prescindia Huntington at the Kirtland Temple (Tullidge, *Women of Mormondom,* 207–8) and John Nicholson ("Temple Manifestations," *Contributor* 16 [1894–95]: 116).

Chapter 10

"REMEMBER THAT YOU DO NOT WALK ALONE"

❧❀❀

How glorious and near to
the angels is youth that is clean.

FIRST PRESIDENCY

President Thomas S. Monson, in addressing the women of the Church in April 2005, gave evidence of his loving nature: "My dear sisters, may God bless you. We love you; we pray for you." President Monson's words reiterated a significant teaching: "Remember that you do not walk alone. The Lord has promised you: 'I will go before your face. I will be on your right hand and on your left, and my Spirit shall be in your hearts, and mine angels round about you, to bear you up.'"[1] In at least three general conference addresses, President Monson has also declared, "How glorious and near to the angels is youth that is clean."[2]

Beyond President Monson's words is the combined testimony

Heber J. Grant, J. Reuben Clark Jr., and David O. McKay, Conference Report, Apr. 1942, 89.

1. "Be Thou an Example," *Ensign*, May 2005, 115.
2. First Presidency [Heber J. Grant, J. Reuben Clark Jr., and David O. McKay], Conference Report, Apr. 1942, 89, cited in Monson, "May You

of prophets and apostles that we do not walk alone in mortality because the Lord's angels frequently visit our sphere of existence, spend time among us, and bless our lives in a variety of ways. Some of these angels are unseen by mortals, choosing to be among us in a state of invisibility or undetectability; others are visible, but their angelic character remains undetected (that is, they appear as mortals); still others appear as angels (perhaps rarely) and reveal their light and glory to those whom they visit. The following general authorities of the Church have taught that angels are in our presence, watching over us:

The Prophet Joseph Smith: "The spirits of the just are exalted to a greater and more glorious work; hence they are blessed in their departure to the World of Spirits. Enveloped in flaming fire *they are not far from us* and know and understand our thoughts and feelings and notions and are *often pained therewith.*"[3]

President Brigham Young: The Lord's "angels are around us . . . There is much in my presence besides those who sit here, if we had eyes to see the heavenly beings that are in our presence."[4]

President Wilford Woodruff: "The angels are watching over us. The eyes of all the heavenly hosts are over us. Those who have lived in other dispensations understand this dispensation far better than we do, and they are watching over the labors of the

Have Courage," *Ensign,* May 2009, 126; "Pathways to Perfection," *Ensign,* May 2002, 100; "Pioneers All," *Ensign,* May 1997, 93.

3. *History of the Church,* 6:51–52.
4. *Discourses of Brigham Young,* 41–42.

Elders of Israel."[5] Also, "angels are watching us and bearing a report of us daily to God."[6]

President Heber C. Kimball: "That is the God whom I serve, one who has millions of angels at His command. Do you suppose that there are any angels here to-day? I would not wonder if there were ten times more angels here than people. We do not see them, but they are here watching us, and are anxious for our salvation."[7] God's "angels are our associates, they are with us and around about us, and watch over us, and take care of us, and lead us, and guide us, and administer to our wants."[8]

Elder Orson Pratt: "There is no doubt . . . that heavenly messengers hover around the congregation of the Saints here assembled . . . God who has seen your labors and diligence in building a house to his name, has no doubt sent heavenly messengers to hover around us, to bluff off the powers of darkness, that seek to darken the minds of the people, and to close their hearts against understanding."[9]

Elder James E. Talmage: Because of God's "great love, He has set heavenly beings to watch over us and to guard us from the attacks of evil powers while we live on earth. Do we realize that in our daily walk and work we are not alone, but that angels attend us wherever our duty causes us to go?"[10]

---

5. Bateman, *Prophets Have Spoken,* 1:1046.
6. Journal, Feb. 13, 1848.
7. *Journal of Discourses,* 3:230.
8. Whitney, *Life of Heber C. Kimball,* 461.
9. *Journal of Discourses,* 19:312–13.
10. *Millennial Star* 55 (July 10, 1893): 446; see also Stuy, *Collected Discourses,* 3:291.

Elder John A. Widtsoe: "Many other intelligent beings, superior to us, no doubt take part in helping man to do his work on earth. There are angels and spirits who, no doubt, have assigned to them the care of the men and women who walk upon earth. Man is not alone; he walks in the midst of such heavenly company, from whom he may expect help if he seek it properly and strongly."[11]

President Harold B. Lee: "When we begin to understand that beyond sight, as Brigham Young said, the spirit world is right here round about us, and if our spiritual eyes could be open, we could see others visiting with us, directing us. And if we will learn not to be so sophisticated that we rule out that possibility of impressions from those who are beyond sight, then we too may have a dream that may direct us as a revelation."[12]

Elder Neal A. Maxwell: "As we take our stand, the faithful will not be alone—not that alone, however. Of necessity, the angel who stood by Christ in Gethsemane to strengthen Him left Him (see Luke 22:43). If we hold aloft the shield of faith in God and faith in His commandments, His angels will be 'round about [us], to bear [us] up' and 'have charge over [us]' (D&C 84:88; D&C 109:22). Of this promise, I testify."[13]

Elder Russell M. Nelson: "Remember, God's holy angels are ever on call to help us. When we are faithful, God and His angels will

---

11. *Rational Theology,* 68.
12. *Stand Ye in Holy Places,* 143.
13. "The Seventh Commandment: A Shield," *Ensign,* Nov. 2001, 80.

help us."[14] Elder Nelson also cited Brigham Young as saying, "All the angels in heaven are looking at this little handful of people, and stimulating them to the salvation of the human family."[15]

President Boyd K. Packer: "If you hold to the rod, you can *feel* your way forward with the gift of the Holy Ghost, conferred upon you at the time you were confirmed a member of the Church. The Holy Ghost will comfort you. You will be able to feel the influence of angels, as Nephi did, and feel your way through life."[16]

In April 1896, President Joseph F. Smith wrote to his missionary son Hyrum Mack Smith to answer his questions about the spirit world. One of Hyrum's questions was "To what extent do our relatives and friends who have died have cognizance of us and our actions?" President Smith's response provides us with great insights with regard to the activities of ministering spirits among mortals. "Now, if our departed kindred and friends are just (righteous) spirits, exalted to this greater and more glorious work, they may be very near us, enveloped in flaming glory, taking notes, or observing actions of our thoughts, feelings, and actions, rejoicing because of our virtues and integrity to the truth, or sorrowing and weeping over our sins and transgressions. And not only so, but able to render assistance, when our spirits are susceptible to the power they wield. . . . I believe that our departed

---

14. "How can I keep from being afraid when scary things happen in the world?" *Friend*, Sept. 2012, 17.
15. *Brigham Young*, 309, 299, cited in Nelson, "Young Adults and the Temple," *Ensign*, Feb. 2006, 15.
16. "Finding Ourselves in Lehi's Dream," *Ensign*, Aug. 2010, 22.

kindred and loved ones are far more mindful of us and solicitous for our salvation day by day than they ever were in the flesh, because they know more."[17]

Twenty years later, near the end of his life, President Smith added this additional witness regarding ministering spirits: "I believe we move and have our being in the presence of heavenly messengers and of heavenly beings. We are not separated from them. . . . I claim that we live in their presence, they see us."[18] These statements from President Joseph F. Smith, together with those of other authoritative witnesses, add crucial understanding that we truly do not walk alone.

President Wilford Woodruff had an experience that pertains to the heavenly hosts who watch over us. In January 1880, he spent ten days with two young sheepherders in the wilderness about forty miles west of Sunset, Arizona. During that time he searched the scriptures, prayed, and sought the will of the Lord. In the night of January 25, he had a vision and a revelation from the Lord, which he recorded at that time: "Thus saith the Lord unto you, my servants and Apostles who dwell in the flesh. Fear ye not your enemies. Let not your hearts be troubled. I am in your midst. I am your advocate with the Father. I have given mine angels charge concerning you. Mine eyes are upon you, and the eyes of your Heavenly Father, and the heavenly hosts and all justified Spirits made perfect are watching over you. Your works are manifest before the face of my servants who have sealed their

---

17. *From Prophet to Son*, 37–39.
18. Conference Report, Apr. 1916, 2–3.

testimony with their blood, and before all my servants of the Apostles whom I have taken unto myself. The veil is taken from off their faces, and they know your works."[19] These words affirm that the Lord and his heavenly host are watching over the Lord's mortal servants and apostles.

Helen Mar Whitney, daughter of Heber C. and Vilate Kimball and mother of Elder Orson F. Whitney, recorded an experience in which she learned that those beyond the veil are aware of us and our needs. Her account was published in the *Woman's Exponent:* "I dreamed, a few nights ago, of being led by circumstances into a room, or office, where I found myself in the presence of a number of our aged brethren, some Apostles, and one brother, who occupied a chair near the centre of the room and attracted my attention most, was from the spirit world . . . After a little he spoke as follows, emphasizing every word so that it impressed itself the stronger upon my memory: 'Why,' said he, 'we are around here all the time, and know everything that is transpiring,' meaning among our own people and the Gentiles, and that there were many more beside himself, who were similarly engaged."[20]

Prophets from our generation have added their witness to these truths. President Ezra Taft Benson taught: "Visitors, seen and unseen, from the world beyond, are often close to us. This is part of eternity which we are living today—part of God's plan. There is no veil to the Lord."[21] And President Harold B. Lee said,

---

19. Journal, Jan. 25, 1880.
20. "Some Serious Reflections," *Woman's Exponent* 17 (Oct. 15, 1888): 73.
21. *Teachings of Ezra Taft Benson,* 35.

"Sometimes we think the whole job is up to us, forgetful that there are loved ones beyond our sight who are thinking about us and our children."[22]

Not only are loved ones near, keeping watch over us and seeking to help us, but Church leaders from the past are doing the same. President Wilford Woodruff spoke of this truth often. In general conference of April 1880 he said: "The eyes of the heavenly hosts are over us; the eyes of God himself and his Son Jesus Christ; the eyes of all the prophets and Apostles who have dwelt in the flesh; they are watching our works. . . . We are not shut out from God, we are not shut out from our brethren, though the vail is between us. They understand our works, our conditions, our position."[23]

This theme occupied President Woodruff's mind during this time in his administration. At the following general conference, President Woodruff continued that theme: "I believe the eyes of the heavenly hosts are over this people," he said. "I believe they are watching the elders of Israel, the prophets and apostles and men who are called to bear off this kingdom. I believe they watch over us all with great interest." President Woodruff provided several examples of those from beyond the veil who had appeared to him:

"After the death of Joseph Smith I saw and conversed with him many times in my dreams in the night season. On one occasion he and his brother Hyrum met me when on the sea going

22. "The Influence and Responsibility of Women," *Relief Society Magazine* 51 (Feb. 1964): 85.
23. Conference Report, Apr. 1880, 9.

on a mission to England . . . [and] the prophet talked freely to me about the mission I was then going to perform. And he also talked to me with regard to the mission of the Twelve Apostles in the flesh, and he laid before me the work they had to perform; and he also spoke of the reward they would receive after death. And there were many other things he laid before me in his interview on that occasion. . . ."

"I have had many interviews with Brother Joseph until the last 15 or 20 years of my life; I have not seen him for that length of time. But during my travels in the southern country last winter I had many interviews with President Young, and with Heber C. Kimball, and Geo. A. Smith, and Jedediah M. Grant, and many others who are dead. They attended our conference, they attended our meetings. And on one occasion, I saw Brother Brigham and Brother Heber ride in [a] carriage ahead of the carriage in which I rode when I was on my way to attend conference; and they were dressed in the most priestly robes. When we arrived at our destination I asked Prest. Young if he would preach to us. He said, 'No, I have finished my testimony in the flesh. I shall not talk to this people any more. But (said he) I have come to see you; I have come to watch over you, and to see what the people are doing. Then (said he) I want you to teach the people—and I want you to follow this counsel yourself—that they must labor and so live as to obtain the Holy Spirit, for without this you cannot build up the kingdom; without the spirit of God you are in danger of walking in the dark, and in danger of failing to accomplish your calling as apostles and as elders in the church and kingdom of God.

And, said he, Brother Joseph taught me this principle.' . . . Do you not think they are interested about us? I tell you they are."[24]

On April 7, 1853, Elder Parley P. Pratt stated that Joseph Smith and others from the world of spirits were present at the laying of the cornerstones of the Salt Lake Temple. "Shall I speak my feelings, that I had on yesterday, while we were laying those Corner Stones of the Temple? Yes, I will utter them, if I can.

"It was not with my eyes, not with the power of actual vision, but by my intellect, by the natural faculties inherent in man, by the exercise of my reason, upon known principles, or by the power of the Spirit, that it appeared to me that Joseph Smith, and his associate spirits, the Latter-day Saints, hovered about us on the brink of that foundation, and with them all the angels and spirits from the other world, that might be permitted, or that were not too busy elsewhere."[25]

At the dedication of the Tokyo Japan Temple, President Spencer W. Kimball remarked, "I expect that every one of the presidents of the Church, all twelve of us, have been dreaming glorious dreams about a temple in Tokyo. This world is not so far from the world of those who have passed on. We feel certain that they are permitted to visit the earth at times, and I think that Joseph Smith, Brigham Young, and all of the presidents, including Heber J. Grant, are surely not far from us this day."[26]

Church leaders from the past also have influence on the Church in the present. After he was called to be an apostle, Elder

24. *Journal of Discourses*, 21:317–18.
25. *Journal of Discourses*, 1:14.
26. *Teachings of Spencer W. Kimball*, 42.

Heber J. Grant struggled mightily with feelings of inadequacy. In his wrestlings, he sought the Lord for solace and reassurance. At one point he was riding alone on horseback. "I seemed to see, and I seemed to hear, what to me is one of the most real things in all my life. I seemed to hear the words that were spoken. I listened to the discussion with a great deal of interest. . . . In this council the Savior was present, my father [Jedediah M. Grant] was there, and the Prophet Joseph Smith was there. . . . It was given to me that the Prophet Joseph Smith and my father mentioned me and requested that I be called to [serve as an apostle]. I sat there and wept for joy. It was given to me that I had done nothing to entitle me to that exalted position, except that I had lived a clean, sweet life. It was given to me that because of my father's having practically sacrificed his life in what was known as the great reformation, so to speak, of the people in early days, having been practically a martyr, that the Prophet Joseph and my father desired me to have that position, and it was because of their faithful labors that I was called, and not because of anything I had done of myself or any great thing that I had accomplished. It was also given to me that that was all these men, the Prophet and my father, could do for me. From that day it depended upon me and upon me alone as to whether I made a success of my life or a failure."[27] This experience convinced Elder Grant that the prophets and apostles in the spirit world still have influence on the workings of the Church in mortality.

---

27. *Gospel Standards,* 195–96.

Chapter 11

ANGELS AND LITTLE CHILDREN

❧❦❧

Our Savior speaks of children and says,
Their angels always stand before my Father.

JOSEPH SMITH

Owing to their innocence and purity, little children enjoy unique privileges with regard to angels. In fact, little children are so significant to God the Father, Jesus Christ, and the kingdom of God on earth that it is possible that they sometimes enjoy the presence of angels; however, because they may not be able to articulate their spiritual experiences nor to write them down for later reading, it is difficult, if not impossible, to know how often they enjoy the ministry of angels. Alma 32:23 states that God "imparteth his word by angels unto men, yea, not only men but women also. Now this is not all; little children do have words given unto them many times, which confound the wise and the learned." Joseph Smith taught that when Jesus "comes to a little child, He will adapt himself to the language and capacity of a little child."[1]

Teachings of the Prophet Joseph Smith, 158.

1. *History of the Church,* 3:392; see also Young, *Journal of Discourses,* 12:174.

Perhaps the same is true of an angel—that he will communicate at the child's level.

Jesus Christ taught his disciples in the Old World the importance of children. His disciples asked him, "Who is the greatest in the kingdom of heaven?" Before responding, Jesus called a child to him, and he set the child in the middle of his disciples. Once Jesus had established this teaching situation, he answered the question: "Except ye be converted, and become as little children, ye shall not enter into the kingdom of heaven." Then Jesus added this doctrine, "Whoso shall offend one of these little ones which believe in me, it were better for him that a millstone were hanged about his neck, and that he were drowned in the depth of the sea." Jesus taught other powerful truths, including the following: "Take heed that ye despise not one of these little ones; for I say unto you, That in heaven their angels do always behold the face of my Father which is in heaven" (Matthew 18:1, 3, 6, 10). When Jesus made the statement that "their angels do always behold the face of my Father," he may have been speaking literally or figuratively or both.

Joseph Smith referred to the passage in Matthew 18 when he taught, "Our Savior speaks of children and says, Their angels always stand before my Father."[2] President George Q. Cannon likewise referenced Matthew 18 regarding the angels who "always behold the face of my father." Writing to readers of the *Juvenile Instructor*, President Cannon explained: "Jesus plainly informs us concerning certain agencies which the Father uses to watch over his little ones—guardian angels, who always behold His face in

---

2. *Teachings of the Prophet Joseph Smith*, 158.

heaven. They watch over those who are put in their charge, and no one can offend or despise them with impunity."[3]

Another scriptural account, 3 Nephi 17:18–24, emphasizes the importance of little children. In this passage, Jesus prayed to the Father, the multitude was "overcome," Jesus stated that his "joy is full," he wept, he blessed the little children "one by one," and he wept a second time. Then ensued one of the most moving and emotional occurrences ever recorded in scripture: The multitude of about twenty-five hundred persons "saw the heavens open, and they saw angels descending out of heaven as it were in the midst of fire; and they came down and encircled those little ones about, and they were encircled about with fire; and the angels did minister unto them."

At general conference, on April 2, 1989, President Ezra Taft Benson addressed little children and promised them that angels would minister to them. He referred to the account from 3 Nephi 17 as one of his "favorite stories" in scripture. After quoting verses 18–24 of that passage, President Benson made a promise: "I promise you, dear children, that angels will minister unto you also. You may not see them, but they will be there to help you, and you will feel of their presence."[4]

In addition to the story in 3 Nephi, there are other stories about angels' ministering to children. For example, an early number of the Church's newspaper *Times and Seasons*, published in

---

3. "God's Care for All His Creations," *Juvenile Instructor* 24 (Jan. 15, 1891): 37.
4. "To the Children of the Church," 5. See also Bateman, *Prophets Have Spoken*, 3:1081.

1844, tells about certain experiences of Nathan Pratt, the young son of the apostle Parley P. Pratt. Nathan "had the gift to discern both good and evil spirits, who sometimes visited him; and on one occasion a kind angel ministered to him, and told him things for his comfort and instruction."[5] Young Nathan died before his sixth birthday.

While serving as the president of the Church, Brigham Young preached a sermon that included a statement about God's angels visiting children. Then-Elder Wilford Woodruff recorded the following from President Young's sermon: "Now look at this building for a school house. The ground around this building should be prepared for a playground and kept neat and clean and prepared so as to make the child happy. Children should be in a clean place. But how is it here? The moment the children step out of door they see nothing but filth all the day long. The minds of our children while young are pure and they should not spend their time in filthy places for it affects their minds and dwellings. They should be in a clean place, for they are visited by the angels of God. But parents do not realize this although it is true."[6]

In an *Ensign* article titled "Sherrie's Shield of Faith," Michael R. Morris related the story of a child named Sherrie, who saw angels in her hospital room as she was recovering from a fourteen-hour operation. Elder Kent F. Richards also recounted Sherrie's experience at general conference in April 2011.[7]

Sherrie's parents, Clayne and Debbie, remained by her

5. "Biography of Nathan Pratt," *Times and Seasons* 5 (Jan. 15, 1844): 414.
6. Journal, Dec. 16, 1855.
7. "The Atonement Covers All Pain," *Ensign*, May 2011, 17.

bedside, praying with all their might that she would survive. When she finally awoke, she began speaking, identifying the angels in the room. "'Daddy, Aunt Cheryl is here,' she told her father. 'And another lady I don't know is with her.'"

For almost an hour Sherrie described visitors from beyond the veil—deceased relatives who had come to comfort her. She mentioned a great-grandfather, a great-great-grandmother, and other deceased loved ones.

At one point she asked, "'Daddy, who is that standing beside you?'

"'I don't know, honey,' Clayne replied. 'Who does he look like?'

"'He looks like you, only taller. . . . He says he's your brother, Jimmy.'

Sherrie had identified Clayne's older brother, Jimmy, who had died of cystic fibrosis when Clayne was three.

"'I doubt that during Sherrie's life Jimmy's name had ever been mentioned,' Clayne says. 'She had never seen a picture of him.'"

Jimmy, along with other deceased family members, visited Sherrie to comfort her. "'People from the other side helped," she observed, "When I was really in pain, they would come and help me calm down. They told me that I would be okay and that I would make it through.'"

Sherrie's experience with angels was not unique. She told her father, "'Daddy, all of the children here in the intensive care unit have angels helping them.'"[8]

---

8. "Sherrie's Shield of Faith," *Ensign*, June 1995, 46.

Chapter 12

ANGELS COMMUNICATE
WITH MORTALS

※⟫⟫⟩ ⟨⟨⟨※

*Should an angel converse with you,
neither you nor he would be confined to corporeal
sight or sound in order to communicate.*

PRESIDENT BOYD K. PACKER

President Boyd K. Packer taught that divine revelation may come in various ways: "The Lord reveals His will through dreams and visions, visitations, through angels, through His own voice, and through the voice of His servants. 'Whether by mine own voice,' He said, 'or by the voice of my servants, it is the same.'"[1] Depending on the needs of mortals and according to the will of the Lord, angels communicate with mortals in a variety of ways—by a visitation, by a voice, by thoughts, by feelings, or in other ways.

"How Does the Spirit Speak to Us?" *New Era*, Feb. 2010, 3; *Mine Errand from the Lord*, 125.

1. "Personal Revelation: The Gift, the Test, and the Promise," *Ensign*, Nov. 1994, 61; see also N. Eldon Tanner, "Warnings from Outer Space," *Ensign*, Nov. 1972, 26: "Since the very beginning of time we have a record of God's messages to man, either by personal appearance, by angels, by direct revelation, by visions, by dreams, or by inspiration."

VISITATIONS OF ANGELS

Both the Bible and the Book of Mormon record a number of examples of angelic visitations. The Bible teaches us that an angel appeared to Hagar (Genesis 16:7–11), Moses (Exodus 3:2), Manoah's wife (Judges 13:3–21), Daniel (Daniel 7:15–16), Ezekiel (Ezekiel 40:1–4), Zechariah (Zechariah 1:9; 2:2–3), Zacharias (Luke 1:11–19), Mary (Luke 1:26–38), Peter (Acts 12:6–10), John (Revelation 17:1, 3, 7; 21:9–27; 22:1–5), and others. The Book of Mormon tells us that an angel appeared to Nephi (1 Nephi 11–14), Laman and Lemuel (1 Nephi 7:10), Alma the Younger (Mosiah 27:11, 14, 18; Alma 36:8, 11; 38:7), individuals from Lamoni's household (Alma 19:34), little children and others in a multitude (3 Nephi 17:18–24), and others.

Angels have also visited many in our dispensation. One such angel is referred to in the following passage: "Verily saith the Lord . . . O inhabitants of the earth, I have sent forth mine angel flying through the midst of heaven, having the everlasting gospel, who hath appeared unto some and hath committed it unto man, who *shall appear unto many that dwell on the earth*" (D&C 133:36; italics added). Elder John A. Widtsoe observed, "Angels have frequently visited men and brought to them divine messages concerning their own affairs or the affairs of the world."[2]

Prophets have testified of angelic visitations. Jacob witnessed, "I truly had seen angels, and they had ministered unto me" (Jacob 7:5). Concerning Nephi's sacred experience, it is written, "Nephi—having been visited by angels . . . having seen angels,

---

2. *Rational Theology,* 71.

and being eye-witness" (3 Nephi 7:15). Gideon also testified, "I have seen an angel of the Lord face to face" (Judges 6:22). Consider also Alma the Younger's testimony, repeated at various times in his life: "For with their own eyes they [the sons of Mosiah] had beheld an angel of the Lord" (Mosiah 27:18); "I arose and stood up, and beheld the angel" (Alma 36:8); and "I have seen an angel face to face, and he spake with me" (Alma 38:7). "And behold, many did declare . . . that they had seen angels and had conversed with them" (Alma 19:34).

Oliver Cowdery, too, bore witness of the reality of an angel's visitation: "The angel of God came down . . . *our eyes beheld—our ears heard.* . . . Then his voice, though mild, pierced to the center, and his words, 'I am thy fellow-servant,' dispelled every fear. We *listened, we gazed,* we admired! 'Twas the voice of an angel from glory—'twas a message from the Most High! and as we heard we rejoiced, while his love enkindled upon our souls, and we were rapt in the vision of the Almighty! Where was room for doubt? No where; uncertainty had fled, doubt had sunk, no more to rise, while fiction and deception had fled forever!"[3]

Most angelic visitations remain private, unknown to the world at large. Joseph Smith explained: "The manifestations of the gift of the Holy Ghost, the ministering of angels, or the development of the power, majesty or glory of God were very seldom manifested publicly, and that generally to the people of God, as to the Israelites; but most generally when angels have come, or God has revealed Himself, it has been to individuals in private,

3. Roberts, *Comprehensive History,* 1:178; italics added.

in their chamber; in the wilderness or fields, and that generally without noise or tumult. The angel delivered Peter out of prison in the dead of night; came to Paul unobserved by the rest of the crew; appeared to Mary and Elizabeth without the knowledge of others; spoke to John the Baptist whilst the people around were ignorant of it.

"When Elisha saw the chariots of Israel and the horsemen thereof, it was unknown to others. When the Lord appeared to Abraham it was at his tent door; when the angels went to Lot, no person knew them but himself."[4]

Many visitations from the spirit world are from relatives, including grandparents, parents, and siblings. Deceased friends, too, may visit loved ones with messages from God. President Joseph F. Smith wrote, "Our fathers and mothers, brothers, sisters and friends who have passed away from this earth, having been faithful, and worthy to enjoy these rights and privileges, may have a mission given them to visit their relatives and friends upon the earth again, bringing from the divine Presence messages of love, of warning, or reproof and instruction, to those whom they had learned to love in the flesh."[5] President Smith then gave an example of Sister Cannon, who "can return and visit her friends," but he added, it had to "be in accordance with the wisdom of the Almighty" because "there are laws to which they who are in the Paradise of God must be subject, as well as laws to which we are subject."[6]

---

4. *History of the Church*, 5:30–31.
5. *Gospel Doctrine*, 436.
6. *Gospel Doctrine*, 436.

DREAMS VERSUS VISIONS

Is there a difference between a vision and an inspired dream? Elder James E. Talmage explained: "In general, visions are manifested to the waking senses whilst dreams are given during sleep. In the vision, however, the senses may be so affected as to render the person practically unconscious, at least oblivious to ordinary occurrences, while he is able to discern the heavenly manifestation. In the earlier dispensations, the Lord frequently communicated through dreams and visions, oftentimes revealing to prophets the events of the future even to the latest generations."[7] Examples of angels communicating with persons in dreams include Jacob ("And the angel of God spake unto me in a dream"; Genesis 31:11), and Joseph ("the angel appeared unto him in a dream"; Matthew 1:20; 2:13, 19).

Some individuals may tend to minimize the significance of dreams originating from God. Some indicate that a vision is greater or more important, but both President Spencer W. Kimball and President Harold B. Lee taught regarding the importance of God-inspired dreams.[8] Even as various persons, both men and women, from the Bible and Book of Mormon had God-inspired dreams and visions that included angels, both men and women in the last days may also experience heavenly communications. Such was the testimony of the prophet Joel (Joel 2:28; see also Acts 2:17). When he visited the young Joseph Smith on the evening of September 21, 1823, the angel Moroni cited Joel

---

7. *Articles of Faith*, 205.
8. Kimball, "The Cause Is Just and Worthy," *Ensign*, May 1974, 119; Lee, *Stand Ye in Holy Places*, 142.

2:28–32 and stated that the words of these verses would soon be fulfilled (see Joseph Smith–History 1:41).

ANGELS COMMUNICATE WITH MORTALS BY SPEAKING TO THEM

We know that angels communicate with mortals by speaking to them. For example, "the angel of the Lord called unto [Abraham] out of heaven . . . the angel of the Lord called unto Abraham out of heaven the second time . . ." (Genesis 22:11, 15). Alma 12:29 states that God "sent angels to converse with them." President Brigham Young told his audience that "there are persons in this congregation that will converse with angels just as freely as we converse with each other."[9]

President Boyd K. Packer, citing passages from the Book of Mormon, explained: "We are told that 'angels speak by the power of the Holy Ghost.' We are even told that when we speak by the power of the Holy Ghost, we 'speak with the tongue [or in the same language] of angels.' (2 Nephi 31:13; 2 Nephi 32:2.)"[10] President Packer further explained: "Nephi explained that angels speak by the power of the Holy Ghost, and you can speak with the tongue of angels, which simply means that you can speak with the power of the Holy Ghost. It will be quiet. It will be invisible. There will not be a dove. There will not be cloven tongues of fire. But the power will be there."[11]

---

9. *Journal of Discourses,* 5:258.

10. "Personal Revelation: The Gift, the Test, and the Promise," *Ensign,* Nov. 1994, 59.

11. "The Gift of the Holy Ghost: What Every Member Should Know," *Ensign,* Aug. 2006, 49–50.

On one occasion, Elder Parley P. Pratt was seeking men to join Zion's Camp; he had traveled for many hours by carriage, ridden through the night, and finally stopped to rest at noon. He loosened the horse to permit it to graze, and then he fell asleep. Because of his exhaustion, he later recorded, he "might have lain in a state of oblivion till the shades of night had gathered about me. . . . I had only slept a few moments till the horse had grazed sufficiently, when a voice, more loud and shrill than I had ever before heard, fell on my ear, and thrilled through every part of my system; it said: *'Parley, it is time to be up and on your journey.'*" Elder Pratt quickly responded, found his horse, and traveled on until he rejoined Zion's Camp. When he told Joseph Smith of this experience, the Prophet explained that it was "the angel of the Lord who went before the camp" who woke him.[12]

ANGELS COMMUNICATE WITH THOUGHTS OR FEELINGS

In addition to angels' visitations and conversations, angels may communicate with thoughts or by feelings. Elder Dallin H. Oaks summarized: "The ministering of angels can also be unseen. Angelic messages can be delivered by a voice or merely by thoughts or feelings communicated to the mind. President John Taylor described 'the action of the angels, or messengers of God, upon our minds, so that the heart can conceive . . . revelations from the eternal world' (*The Gospel Kingdom,* sel. G. Homer Durham [1943], 31).

"Nephi described three manifestations of the ministering of angels when he reminded his rebellious brothers that (1) they

---

12. *Autobiography,* 93–94.

had 'seen an angel,' (2) they had 'heard his voice from time to time,' and (3) also that an angel had 'spoken unto [them] in a still small voice' though they were 'past feeling' and 'could not feel his words' (1 Nephi 17:45) . . . Most angelic communications are felt or heard rather than seen."[13]

As Elder Oaks attested, mortals can *feel* the words of an angel. The full text of 1 Nephi 17:45 states: "Ye are swift to do iniquity but slow to remember the Lord your God. Ye have seen an angel, and he spake unto you; yea, ye have heard his voice from time to time; and he hath spoken unto you in a still small voice, *but ye were past feeling, that ye could not feel* his words; wherefore, he has spoken unto you like unto the voice of thunder, which did cause the earth to shake as if it were to divide asunder" (italics added). The concept of feeling an angel's words may be indicated in the following passage from latter-day scripture: "Which our forefathers have awaited with anxious expectation to be revealed in the last times, *which their minds were pointed to by the angels,* as held in reserve for the fulness of their glory" (D&C 121:27; italics added).

ANGELS CAN GIVE IMPRESSIONS

Christopher Columbus was guided by an angel from the Lord, who "gave him deep impressions," taught Elder Orson Hyde on America's Independence Day in 1854: "[An] angel was with Columbus, and gave him deep impressions, by dreams and by visions, respecting this New World. Trammelled by poverty and by an unpopular cause, yet his persevering and unyielding

---

13. "The Aaronic Priesthood and the Sacrament," *Ensign,* Nov. 1998, 38–39.

heart would not allow an obstacle in his way too great for him to overcome; and the angel of God helped him."[14]

ANGELS CAN COMMUNICATE THROUGH PURE INTELLIGENCE

Other Church authorities provide additional understanding regarding spiritual communications with angels. President Boyd K. Packer, citing the Prophet Joseph Smith, referred to "pure intelligence," which one may experience when communicating with an angel: "Should an angel converse with you, neither you nor he would be confined to corporeal sight or sound in order to communicate. For there is that spiritual process described by the Prophet Joseph by which pure intelligence can flow into our minds and by which we can know what we need to know without either the effort of study or the passage of time, because that is revelation."[15]

LAWS GOVERN ANGELS AND THEIR COMMUNICATIONS

Angels' visitations and communications must be authorized by those authorities who are assigned to direct such work. All of God's messengers, whether they are resurrected or translated beings, unembodied or disembodied spirits, or mortals must comply with God's laws relating to communication among the different spheres of existence. The Prophet Joseph Smith taught that "the organization of the spiritual and heavenly worlds, and of spiritual and heavenly beings, was agreeable to the most perfect order and harmony: their limits and bounds were fixed irrevocably."[16]

---

14. *Journal of Discourses,* 6:368.
15. *Mine Errand from the Lord,* 125.
16. *Teachings of the Prophet Joseph Smith,* 325.

Without order and divine organization among the spheres, there would exist chaos and confusion. Elder Orson F. Whitney explained: "God's house is a house of order, and the spirit world is a room in that house. This being the case, it is only reasonable to conclude that before anything important or unusual can take place there, the Master of the Mansion must first give consent. Otherwise confusion would prevail, and the divine purpose for which the veil was dropped between the two worlds might be thwarted. . . . Permission from the Great Father would have to be obtained before one of his children, either an unembodied or a disembodied spirit, could make itself manifest to mortals."[17]

---

17. *Saturday Night Thoughts*, 307.

Chapter 13

"CARRIED BY THE ANGELS INTO ABRAHAM'S BOSOM"

※◈※ ◈ ◈◈◈

A certain beggar named Lazarus . . . died, and
was carried by the angels into Abraham's bosom.

LUKE 16:20–22

One who has passed from mortality may visit a mortal to inform that person that he or she will soon depart from this life. President Ezra Taft Benson tells the story of his deceased father-in-law, Carl Christian Amussen, who appeared to his wife, Barbara Smith Amussen, to tell her of her approaching death. "This choice woman knew the exact time she was to depart mortal life. Her husband, a Danish convert and Utah's first pioneer jeweler and watchmaker, Carl Christian Amussen, appeared to her in either a dream or a vision. She admitted, 'I'm not sure which, but it was so real it seemed that he was right in the room. He said he had come to tell me that my time in mortal life was ending and that on the following Thursday [it was then Friday], I would be expected to leave mortal life.'"

Sister Amussen was convinced that her husband had appeared to her and that she would pass away the following Thursday. As a result, she made concrete plans: On Sunday at Church, she bore her testimony and bade the ward members good-bye. During the following days, she withdrew her savings from the bank, ordered her casket from a local mortuary, paid her bills, and even had the power and water turned off at her home. Then she went to the home of her daughter Mabel to await her passing. Sister Amussen did die that Thursday, just as her deceased husband had told her. President Benson recounted, "On the day of her passing, Mabel came into the room where her mother was reclining on the bed. Her mother said, 'Mabel, I feel a little bit drowsy. I feel I will go to sleep. Do not disturb me if I sleep until the eventide.'

"Those were her last words, and she peacefully passed away."[1]

A second example of a messenger who visited a mortal to inform him that he would soon depart from this life is recorded in the biography of President Heber C. Kimball, wherein Elder Orson F. Whitney wrote that the angel Moroni visited Heber to notify him of his imminent death: "At family prayers, just a little while before his death, he remarked that the angel Moroni had visited him the night before and informed him that his work on this earth was finished, and he would soon be taken."[2]

These two accounts may not exemplify common occurrences; we simply do not know how often spirits or angels visit loved ones shortly before death. Beyond these two accounts, however, there are other documented reports of angels who came to receive individuals near or at the time of their death, including reports by

1. *Come unto Christ*, 21–22.
2. *Life of Heber C. Kimball*, 442.

the Prophet Joseph Smith, President Heber C. Kimball, President Wilford Woodruff, and President Rudger Clawson. As we examine these reports, we should keep in mind that we are not always certain when those who relate the reports are using figures of speech or symbolic expressions rather than literal statements that describe actual events.

A well-known example of angels receiving a mortal at death is recorded in the parable of the rich man and Lazarus (Luke 16:19–31), in which "a certain beggar named Lazarus . . . died, and was carried by the angels into Abraham's bosom" (Luke 16:20–22). The expression "Abraham's bosom" refers to paradise or the world of spirits. The words "carried by the angels" may be symbolic (Lazarus's spirit proceeded to the world of spirits) or literal (angels actually accompanied Lazarus into the world of spirits). Moreover, we must remember this story of Lazarus and the rich man is a parable, and parables do not establish doctrines of the Church.

President Rudger Clawson, during the 1925 April general conference, spoke of "the angel of death," but he was not referring to a destroying angel: "Brother, . . . the angel of death may have been in your father's home when he passed away, in fact, may have come for your father, but he was not a destroying angel, no, he was an angel of peace, of mercy, of hope, of love, and he came to open the door of light and life and everlasting joy to your good father."[3] President Clawson's statement reminds us that the angel of death may be a messenger of peace and love who opens

---

3. Conference Report, Apr. 1925, 62.

the door to light and joy. Besides President Clawson's account, President Wilford Woodruff once related a story about a dying man and an angel of death.[4]

Joseph Smith made a statement regarding the Lord's angel and the death of his oldest brother, Alvin: "He was one of the soberest of men, and when he died the angel of the Lord visited him in his last moments."[5]

On August 10, 1840, Seymour Brunson, a resident of Nauvoo who served as a member of the high council, passed away. About a month later, on September 6, 1840, Vilate Kimball wrote a letter to her husband, Heber C. Kimball, regarding Brother Brunson's death: "Seymour Brunson is . . . dead, everything was done to save him that could be done, but the Lord had need of him. A short time before he died he told Joseph not to hold him any longer 'for' said he, 'I have seen David Patten and he wants me, and the Lord wants me, and I want to go.' They then gave him up; at one time as Joseph entered the room, he told him that there was a light encircled him above the brightness of the sun— he exclaimed, 'The room is full of angels they have come to waft my spirit home.' He then bade his family and friends farewell and sweetly fell asleep in Jesus."[6]

A couple of months later, on November 9, 1840, Heber C. Kimball wrote to John Taylor and told how David Patten and a number of angels had come to take Brunson home. Elder

---

4. See *Deseret Weekly* 53 (Nov. 7, 1896): 642; see also Stuy, *Collected Discourses,* 5:235.
5. *History of the Church,* 5:127.
6. Holzapfel and Holzapfel, *Woman's View,* 175.

Kimball wrote: "Seymour Brunson is gone. David Patten came after him. The room was full of angels that came after him to waft him home, he was buried under arms. The procession, that went to the grave was judged to be one mile long, and a more joyful season she [Vilate Kimball] says she never saw before on the account of the glory that Joseph set forth."[7] A parallel account states: "Colonel Seymour Brunson, one of the first elders in the Church, who had always been a 'lively stone in the building of the Kingdom God,' died in 'triumph of faith,' at the age of 40. John Smith writing his son George A., serving as a missionary in England, mentioned the death of Elder Brunson. 'He died very happy,' he wrote, 'David Patten came after him, he said, with a convoy of angels.'"[8]

President Wilford Woodruff told of a remarkable experience that occurred when "two personages came into the room" to receive his wife, who had died minutes before. Through President Woodruff's faith and priesthood administration and through the exercise of agency by his wife, however, she was restored to life, and the two personages departed.[9]

At general conference in the Tabernacle in Salt Lake City, President Wilford Woodruff related another account wherein someone from the world of spirits came to receive a mortal at death. President Woodruff told of a deceased man named Peter Maughan, who had appeared to three mortals with the goal of appointing one of them to die. Peter went to the first man and

---

7. Ehat and Cook, *Words of Joseph Smith*, 49n1; spelling standardized.
8. Barrett, *Joseph Smith and the Restoration*, 413.
9. See *Leaves from My Journal*, 96–97.

conversed with him but concluded that he would not "call" that man to come to the other side of the veil. Peter then went to the second man, who, like the first, was not taken in death. The third man, days later, "was taken sick and died." President Woodruff concluded: "Now, I name this to show a principle. They have work on the other side of the vail; and they want men, and they call them. And that was my view in regard to Brother George A. Smith. When he was almost at death's door, Brother Cannon administered to him, and in thirty minutes he was up and ate breakfast with his family. We labored with him in this way, but ultimately, as you know, he died. But it taught me a lesson. I felt that man was wanted behind the vail."[10]

President Heber J. Grant related a story regarding his seven-year-old son, who died from a hip disease. President Grant's deceased wife, the mother of the boy, came for him, together with a messenger from the eternal world: "About an hour before he died I had a dream that his mother, who was dead, came for him, and that she brought with her a messenger, and she told this messenger to take the boy while I was asleep." About that time, Heber's brother, who was present in the house, awakened him. Heber recorded that his brother "called me into the room and told me that my child was dying.

"I went in the front room and sat down. There was a vacant chair between me and my wife who is now living, and I felt the presence of that boy's deceased mother, sitting in that chair. I did

---

10. *Journal of Discourses*, 22:334. President Woodruff may have known that angels would receive him at his own death; see Journal, Jan. 25, 1880.

not tell anybody what I felt, but I turned to my living wife and said: 'Do you feel anything strange?' She said: 'Yes, I feel assured that Heber's mother is sitting between us, waiting to take him away.'"

Because of this extraordinary spiritual experience, Heber was able to find peace when his son passed away. "My living wife, my brother, and I, upon that occasion experienced a sweet, peaceful, and heavenly influence in my home, as great as I have ever experienced in my life."[11]

The following accounts suggest that the Prophet Joseph Smith, and Hyrum also, in one another account, came back to welcome or accompany loved ones to the spirit world. The first account pertains to Joseph's beloved wife Emma, and the second deals with Brigham Young, who eventually succeeded him as president of the Church.

Shortly before Emma Hale Smith Bidamon's death on April 30, 1879, the Prophet Joseph apparently came for her. "During the night Joseph and Alexander [Emma's sons] alternated turns at Emma's bedside. Alexander heard her call, 'Joseph, Joseph, Joseph,' and wakened his brother. Joseph hurried into the room to see his mother raise herself up and extend her left arm. 'Joseph!' they heard her say. 'Yes, yes, I'm coming.'

"Alexander slipped his arm behind her shoulders and grasped her hand.

"'Mother, what is it?' he asked. But Emma did not answer. He folded her hand against her breast and laid her back. At twenty

---

11. *Gospel Standards*, 364–65.

minutes after four in the early dawn of April 30, 1879, Emma was dead."[12]

Susa Young Gates and Leah D. Widtsoe told of Brigham Young's last words before he passed away: When Brigham "was placed upon the bed in front of the window he seemed to partially revive, and opening his eyes, he gazed upward, exclaiming: 'Joseph! Joseph! Joseph!' and the divine look in his face seemed to indicate that he was communicating with his beloved friend, Joseph Smith, the Prophet. This name was the last word he uttered."[13]

Alexander Neibaur had the following experience: Shortly before his death, "his face suddenly lit up and his countenance brightened. He cast his eyes upward as if he could see far into upper distant spaces.

"'What do you see, father?' [his daughters] asked. The dying man murmured clearly, 'Joseph—Hyrum—' then his weary eyes closed forever."[14]

12. Newell and Avery, *Mormon Enigma*, 304.
13. Gates and Widtsoe, *Life Story of Brigham Young*, 362.
14. "Alexander Neibaur," *Utah Genealogical and Historical Magazine*, Apr. 1914, 62.

Chapter 14

ANGELS SERVE AS GUIDES AND INTERPRETERS TO PROPHETS

✦❈✦

The angel said unto me: Behold the Lamb of God,
yea, even the Son of the Eternal Father! Knowest
thou the meaning of the tree which thy father saw?

1 NEPHI 11:21

Angels may serve as guides and interpreters to God's prophets; incidents of angels serving as guides are attested in the Old and New Testaments, in the Book of Mormon, and in our dispensation, we have record that an angel served as a guide to President Wilford Woodruff.

AN ANGEL SHOWS JERUSALEM'S FUTURE TEMPLE TO EZEKIEL

During his captivity in Babylon, Ezekiel received a vision of Jerusalem's future temple, which vision spans eight chapters in his record (Ezekiel 40–47). At the beginning of his vision, Ezekiel told of an angel who served as his guide: "Behold, there was a man, whose appearance was like the appearance of brass, with a line of flax in his hand, and a measuring reed; and he stood in the gate" (Ezekiel 40:3).

The angel's part in the vision was not passive or secondary; he had an active role. The angel escorted the prophet from place to place in and around the future temple. On twenty-six occasions Ezekiel wrote that the angel "brought me," "he brought me," or "brought he me" from one place to the next. "Then brought he me into the outward court" (Ezekiel 40:17), "and he brought me to the inner court" (Ezekiel 40:28), and so forth.

This angel had two measuring tools in his hand, a line of flax and a measuring reed. The length of the line of flax is now unknown, but the measuring reed was nine to ten feet long. With the reed, the angel measured various architectural components of the temple. At least thirty-three times, the text states, the angel measured this or that component. For instance, "he measured the posts thereof and the arches thereof" (Ezekiel 40:24), "he measured the court" (Ezekiel 40:47), and so forth. Each time the angel measured something, Ezekiel was required to write the measurement down. The angel used the line of flax to measure the depth of water which flowed from the temple (see Ezekiel 47:3–5).

DANIEL'S VISION IN DANIEL 7

Daniel 7 records a vision that may be divided into three parts: First, Daniel sees four ferocious creatures—a lion, a bear, a leopard, and an unnamed beast (Daniel 7:1–8); second, the council at Adam-ondi-Ahman (Daniel 7:9–14); and third, the interpretation of the dream (Daniel 7:15–28). Daniel's entire vision is full of symbolism. Perhaps because of the symbolism, Daniel sought understanding from one of the heavenly attendants who was standing nearby, and he received the interpretation, recorded in Daniel 7:16–27. The attendant remains unnamed, although it may have been Gabriel (see Daniel 8:16).

THE ANGEL GABRIEL INTERPRETS DANIEL'S VISION OF THE RAM AND THE GOAT

During the third year of King Belshazzar's reign, Daniel received a vision of a ram and a goat (Daniel 8:1–27). At the conclusion of the vision, which contains many symbolic elements, Daniel "sought for the meaning" (Daniel 8:15). In response, the angel Gabriel appeared to the prophet. Daniel wrote that Gabriel "came near where I stood. . . . And he said, Behold, I will make thee know what shall be in the last end of the indignation" (Daniel 8:17–19). After Gabriel explained the meaning of the vision (see Daniel 8:19–25), he bore witness that "the vision . . . is true" (Daniel 8:26).

ZECHARIAH'S EIGHT VISIONS AND THE ANGELS WHO INTERPRETED THEM

Zechariah 1–6 features eight visions of the prophet Zechariah: a man on a red horse with other horses (Zechariah 1:7–17); four horns and four carpenters (Zechariah 1:18–21); a man with a measuring line (Zechariah 2:1–13); Joshua, the high priest (Zechariah 3:1–10); a golden lampstand and two olive trees (Zechariah 4:1–14); a flying scroll (Zechariah 5:1–4); a woman and a basket (Zechariah 5:5–11); and four chariots (Zechariah 6:1–8). The eight visions contain many symbols, which may have prompted Zechariah to ask an angel for the meaning of the vision.

For the first vision, Zechariah inquired of the angel by asking, "What are these?" and "the angel that talked with me said unto me, I will shew thee what these be" (Zechariah 1:9). For the second vision, the prophet "said unto the angel that talked with me, What be these?" and the angel provided an answer (Zechariah 1:19–21). And so continued the angelic instruction to the prophet Zechariah (see Zechariah 2:1–13; 3:1–10; 4:1–14; 5:5–11; 6:1–8).

AN ANGEL SHOWS JOHN THE GREAT WHORE UPON THE WATERS

John wrote, "And there came one of the seven angels which had the seven vials, and talked with me, saying unto me, Come hither; I will shew unto thee the judgment of the great whore that sitteth upon many waters" (Revelation 17:1). Then the angel carried John "away in the spirit into the wilderness" (v. 3). During this vision, the angel served as an interpreter to John regarding things that he had seen in his vision. The angel informed John, "I will tell thee the mystery of the woman, and of the beast that carrieth her, which hath the seven heads and ten horns" (v. 7). The angel's interpretation is recorded in Revelation 17:7–18.

AN ANGEL SHOWS JOHN THE NEW JERUSALEM

One of the angels that poured plagues from the seven bowls (see Revelation 16:1–21) spoke to John and said, "Come hither, I will shew thee the bride, the Lamb's wife." And then the angel "carried [John] away in the spirit to a great and high mountain, and shewed [him] that great city, the holy Jerusalem, descending out of heaven from God" (Revelation 21:9–10).

In sum, the angel showed to John regarding the New Jerusalem that the city, the holy celestial city, will send forth a wonderful light. It will have high walls with foundations made of precious stones, and its gates will be made of pearl and guarded by twelve angels. The city itself will be "pure gold, like unto clear glass." Within the city will be a "pure river of water of life" and "the tree of life." The inhabitants of the city will dwell in the presence of God, "and they shall see his face, . . . and they shall reign for ever and ever" (Revelation 21:18; 22:1–2, 4–5).

An angel guides and instructs Nephi

Chapters 11–14 of 1 Nephi set forth a grand vision received by Nephi, wherein an angel serves as his guide and instructor. "And it came to pass that I saw the heavens open; and an angel came down and stood before me" (1 Nephi 11:14). The angel, who is not named, instructed Nephi concerning a number of sacred doctrines pertaining to Mary, the mother of Jesus; the condescension of God; Jesus's baptism, reception of the Holy Ghost, healings, and crucifixion; and much more. Nephi also envisioned many things concerning the land of promise, the church of the devil, the Bible, and the latter-day Zion.

This angel plays a prominent role in Nephi's vision. The word *angel* is found thirty-five times in 1 Nephi 11–14. Nephi and the angel interact so often throughout the vision that on thirty-two occasions Nephi stated that "the angel spake unto me" (or a similar form of this phrase). In other words, the angel continually served as Nephi's instructor during the vision. Nephi would see something in the vision, and the angel would then explain what Nephi was seeing.

Furthermore, while teaching Nephi, the angel demonstrated that he (the angel) was an experienced master teacher. For example, he used exclamations such as "Look!" (nine times) or "Behold" (sixteen times); both of these exclamations (and others) are effective rhetorical tools. The angel also employed questions (another excellent teaching technique) to prompt Nephi to consider certain points of the vision. These questions include the following: "Knowest thou the meaning of the tree which thy father saw?" (1 Nephi 11:21); "What beholdest thou?" (1 Nephi 13:2); "Knowest thou the meaning of the book?" (1 Nephi 13:21); and "Rememberest thou the covenants of the Father unto the house of Israel?" (1 Nephi 14:8). These questions prompted Nephi to consider what he was seeing in the vision and then to respond.

Nephi concluded his record of this vision with a testimony of the angel's role during the vision: "And I bear record that I saw the things which my father saw, and the angel of the Lord did make them known unto me" (1 Nephi 14:29).

AN ANGEL GUIDES AND INSTRUCTS WILFORD WOODRUFF

President Wilford Woodruff, like the prophets of old, had a vision wherein an angel appeared to him and showed him many of the scenes that would take place in the last days. This vision took place in 1835, while Wilford was in Tennessee at the home of Abraham O. Smoot:

"I received a letter from Brothers Joseph Smith and Oliver Cowdery, requesting me to stay there, and stating that I would lose no blessing by doing so. Of course, I was satisfied . . . while I rejoiced in this letter and the promise made to me, I became wrapped in vision. I was like Paul; I did not know whether I was in the body or out of the body. A personage appeared to me and showed me the great scenes that should take place in the last days. One scene after another passed before me. I saw the sun darkened; I saw the moon become as blood; I saw the stars fall from heaven; I saw seven golden lamps set in the heavens, representing the various dispensations of God to man—a sign that would appear before the coming of Christ. I saw the resurrection of the dead . . . if I had been an artist I could have painted the whole scene as it was impressed upon my mind, more indelibly fixed than anything I had ever seen with the natural eye."[1]

---

1. *Deseret Weekly* 53 (Nov. 7, 1896): 642.

Chapter 15

ANGELS REVEAL TRUTHS TO GOD'S PROPHETS

✦❧✦ ✦❧✦

Joseph Smith . . . truly looked into
the heavens and communed with God the
Father and the Son and with angels.

PRESIDENT DIETER F. UCHTDORF

Elder Neal A. Maxwell explained that there is a "particular pattern of divine instruction" when the gospel is restored on the earth. This pattern includes God sending angels to his prophet. "The glorious things restored in the nineteenth century," wrote Elder Maxwell, "included the calling of a prophet, Joseph Smith, who heard God's own voice, received angelic revelations and also the holy apostleship and priesthood keys."[1]

Our prophets, seers, and revelators indeed have the right and privilege of receiving revelation for the entire Church through visitations by angels and other means. In April 1830, the Lord spoke to the Prophet Joseph Smith regarding "the revelations of

"We Are Doing a Great Work and Cannot Come Down," *Ensign*, May 2009, 62.

1. "From the Beginning," *Ensign*, Oct. 1993, 19.

God which shall come hereafter by the gift and power of the Holy Ghost, the voice of God, or the ministering of angels" (D&C 20:35). Although only few of many, the following accounts demonstrate that angels reveal truths and doctrines to God's prophets.

The Church was restored in this dispensation in part because angels revealed truths and ordinances to the Prophet Joseph Smith. One Church history scholar has documented seventy-six of Joseph's "visionary experiences." Many of these visionary experiences involved angels:

- Many angels (spring 1820)
- Moroni (multiple visitations) (Sept. 21–22, 1823)
- "Ancient inhabitants of 'this country'" (Sept. 21–22, 1823)
- Many angels (Sept. 22, 1823–Sept. 22, 1827)
- Moroni ("three annual intervals") (Sept. 22, 1824–Sept. 22, 1826)
- Moroni "instructed Joseph Smith near the Hill Cumorah" (early 1827)
- Moroni "delivered the plates and sacred relics to Joseph Smith" (Sept. 22, 1827)
- "Moroni took the Urim and Thummim from Joseph Smith" (June–July 1828)
- "Moroni returned the Urim and Thummim" (June–July 1828)
- "Moroni took the plates and, again, the Urim and Thummim" (summer 1828)
- "Moroni returned the plates and the Urim and Thummim" (Sept. 22, 1828)
- John the Baptist (May 15, 1829)
- Peter, James, and John (May–June 1829)
- Moroni (on three different occasions) (May–June 1829)

- An angel showed Joseph, Oliver Cowdery, and David Whitmer the plates and sacred relics (June 1829)
- An angel showed Joseph and Martin Harris the plates and sacred relics (June 1829)
- Moroni (twice) (June 1829)
- An angel gave Joseph a revelation on the sacrament (Aug. 1830)
- Jehovah and Adam at Adam-ondi-Ahman (Dec. 18, 1833)
- Adam and Eve (April 18, 1834)
- Some inhabitants of the celestial kingdom (Jan. 21, 1836)
- Many angels in the Kirtland Temple, including Peter (Mar. 27, 1836)
- John the Beloved and other angels in the Kirtland Temple (Mar. 30, 1836)
- Moses, Elijah, and Elias in the Kirtland Temple (Apr. 3, 1836)
- An angel carried away William Marks (Mar. 1838)
- An angel (at least three times) who commanded Joseph to practice plural marriage (before 1843)[2]

A passage in the Doctrine and Covenants encapsulates what knowledge these and other angels imparted to the Prophet: "And the voice of Michael, the archangel; the voice of Gabriel, and of Raphael, and of divers angels, from Michael or Adam down to the present time, all declaring their dispensation, their rights, their keys, their honors, their majesty and glory, and the power of their priesthood" (D&C 128:21). Elder Dallin H. Oaks observed:

---

2. Baugh, "Parting the Veil," in Welch and Carlson, *Opening the Heavens*, 265–326.

"The Prophet Joseph had no role models from whom he could learn how to be a prophet and leader of the Lord's people. He learned from heavenly messengers and from the harvest of his unique spiritual gifts."[3]

The Prophet no doubt received additional communications from other heavenly beings. Some thirty-five years after the Prophet's martyrdom, President John Taylor taught: "The principles which he [Joseph Smith] had, placed him in communication with the Lord, and not only with the Lord, but with the ancient apostles and prophets; such men, for instance, as Abraham, Isaac, Jacob, Noah, Adam, Seth, Enoch, and Jesus and the Father, and the apostles that lived on this continent as well as those who lived on the Asiatic continent. He seemed to be as familiar with these people as we are with one another. Why? Because he had to introduce a dispensation which was called the dispensation of the fulness of times, and it was known as such by the ancient servants of God."[4]

President Taylor's statement that Joseph Smith "seemed to be as familiar with these people as we are with one another" is borne out by other recorded statements. On one occasion Joseph visited his sister Catherine Smith Salisbury in Illinois; this gave him time to reflect on his family, especially his deceased brother Alvin. He wrote that "the circumstance brought vividly to my mind many things pertaining to my father's house, of which I spake freely, and particularly of my brother Alvin. He was a very handsome man,

---

3. "Joseph, the Man and the Prophet," *Ensign,* May 1996, 72.
4. *Journal of Discourses,* 21:94.

surpassed by none but Adam and Seth, and of great strength."[5] Joseph's ability to compare Alvin's appearance to that of Adam and Seth suggests that Joseph had at some point in time seen those two ancient individuals in vision. On another occasion, "Joseph Smith said that our old father Adam was such a perfect man great and stout, that he never stumbled or fell a joint to the ground."[6]

Joseph Smith did indeed see Adam in vision, perhaps on more than one occasion. Zebedee Coltrin recorded a visionary experience that involved himself, Joseph Smith, and Oliver Cowdery. Zebedee wrote that he "noticed that Joseph seemed to have a far off look in his eyes, or was looking at a distance. Presently he stepped between Brothers Cowdery and me, and taking us by the arm said, 'Let's take a walk.'" They went to a place where there was grass, birch, and grape vines. Joseph Smith then instructed, "'Let us pray.'" They all three prayed in turn—Joseph, Oliver and Zebedee. Joseph then said, "'Now brethren, we will see some visions.' . . .

"The heavens gradually opened, and we saw a golden throne, on a circular foundation, and on the throne sat a man and a woman, having white hair and clothed in white garments. Their heads were white as snow, and their faces shone with immortal youth. They were the two most beautiful and perfect specimens of mankind I ever saw. Joseph said, 'They are our first parents, Adam and Eve.'

---

5. *History of the Church*, 5:247.
6. *Selected Writings of Robert J. Matthews*, 135–36.

"Adam was a large broad shouldered man, and Eve, as a woman, was as large in proportion."[7]

Lucy Mack Smith affirmed that Joseph was so familiar with "the ancient inhabitants of this continent" that he could describe their customs, clothing, cities, practices of worship and much more. Apparently, Joseph saw these inhabitants and their customs in vision. Lucy wrote that Joseph "would describe the ancient inhabitants of this continent, their dress, mode of travelling, and the animals upon which they rode; their cities, their buildings, with every particular; their mode of warfare; and also their religious worship. This he would do with as much ease, seemingly, as if he had spent his whole life with them."[8]

Sometime during the early part of August 1830, Newel Knight and his wife, Sally Colburn Knight, visited Joseph and Emma Smith at Harmony, Pennsylvania. Joseph decided that the two couples would partake of the sacrament together. Joseph therefore left to obtain wine for the sacrament, but soon after he left a heavenly messenger appeared to him. He recorded, "I set out to procure some wine for the occasion, but had gone only a short distance when I was met by a heavenly messenger, and received the following revelation [D&C 27]."[9]

Prophets since Joseph Smith have also received angelic visitations. On Tuesday, February 23, 1847, Brigham Young said to

---

7. Dahl and Cannon, *Encyclopedia of Joseph Smith's Teachings,* 18.
8. Baugh, "Parting the Veil," in Welch and Carlson, *Opening the Heavens,* 271. A letter written by Helen Mar Whitney tells of a visit of a Nephite to Joseph Smith; see Holzapfel and Holzapfel, *Woman's View,* 173.
    9. *History of the Church,* 1:106.

members of the Quorum of the Twelve: "I dreamed that I went to . . . Joseph [Smith]. He looked perfectly natural . . ." President Young gave details of this dream and then explained that Joseph had instructed him to "tell the people to be humble and faithful, and be sure to keep the spirit of the Lord and it will lead them right. Be careful and not turn away the small still voice; it will teach you what to do and where to go; it will yield the fruits of the kingdom. Tell the brethren to keep their hearts open to conviction, so that when the Holy Ghost comes to them, their hearts will be ready to receive it. They can tell the Spirit of the Lord from all other spirits; it will whisper peace and joy to their souls; it will take malice, hatred, strife and all evil from their hearts; and their whole desire will be to do good, bring forth righteousness and build up the kingdom of God."[10]

Elder Jeffrey R. Holland retold another dream Brigham Young received: "Before leaving Nauvoo in the winter of 1846, President Brigham Young had a dream in which he saw an angel standing on a cone-shaped hill somewhere in the West pointing to a valley below." About a year and a half later, when Brigham arrived in the Salt Lake Valley, he saw the cone-shaped hill and the valley below it and recognized that this scene was that which the angel had revealed. The hill was later named Ensign Peak, because Brigham, along with other leaders, planted a homemade flag, or ensign, on its summit.[11] His dream of the angel standing

---

10. Watson, *Manuscript History of Brigham Young*, 528–30; see also McConkie, *Angels*, 98–99. Wilford Woodruff mentions this account in one of his sermons; see *Deseret Weekly* 53 (Nov. 7, 1896), 643.

11. "An Ensign to the Nations," *Ensign*, May 2011, 111; see also the account

on the hill led to the Latter-day Saints settling in the Salt Lake Valley. Today, the Saints together with their temples, chapels, and homes fill that valley and beyond.

Angels have also revealed sacred truths to others. President Wilford Woodruff recorded: "Joseph Smith visited me a great deal after his death, and taught me many important principles. The last time he visited me was while I was in a storm at sea. . . . Joseph and Hyrum visited me, and the Prophet laid before me a great many things. Among other things, he told me to get the Spirit of God; that all of us needed it. He also told me what the Twelve Apostles would be called to go through on the earth before the coming of the Son of Man, and what the reward of their labors would be."[12]

In a momentous talk about angels, published November 7, 1896, President Woodruff taught: "I have referred to the administration of angels to myself. What did these angels do? One of them taught me some things relating to the signs that should precede the coming of the Son of Man."[13]

President Woodruff once explained to the Saints that Joseph Smith, after his death, revealed significant truths to him about why he and others were actively preparing for Jesus Christ's second coming: "In the night vision I saw [Joseph Smith] at the door of the temple in heaven. He came to me and spoke to me. He said he could not stop to talk with me because he was in a hurry. The next man I met was Father Smith; he could not talk with me because he

---

of George A. Smith, *Journal of Discourses,* 13:85.

12. *Discourses of Wilford Woodruff,* 288.

13. *Deseret Weekly* 53 (Nov. 7, 1896), 643; see also Stuy, *Collected Discourses,* 5:238.

was in a hurry. I met half a dozen brethren who had held high positions on earth, and none of them could stop to talk with me because they were in a hurry. I was much astonished. By and by I saw the Prophet again and I got the privilege of asking him a question. 'Now,' said I, 'I want to know why you are in a hurry. I have been in a hurry all through my life; but I expected my hurry would be over when I got into the kingdom of heaven, if I ever did.'

"Joseph said: 'I will tell you, Brother Woodruff. Every dispensation that has had the priesthood on the earth and has gone into the celestial kingdom, has had a certain amount of work to do to prepare to go to the earth with the Savior when He goes to reign on the earth. Each dispensation has had ample time to do this work. We have not. We are the last dispensation, and so much work has to be done, and we need to be in a hurry in order to accomplish it.' Of course, that was satisfactory, but it was new doctrine to me."[14]

Other deceased Church leaders visited President Woodruff and revealed truths to him: "I have had many interviews with President Young since he died, a great many teachings from him, and from others who held important positions here in the flesh, but who have gone into the spirit world, and seem, in a measure, to have an interest and watch-care over the Church and Kingdom of God though they have passed to the other side of the veil."[15] President Woodruff testified, "I have had many interviews with Brother Joseph until the last 15 or 20 years of my life; . . . during my

14. *Deseret Weekly* 53 (Nov. 7, 1896): 642–43; see also Stuy, *Collected Discourses,* 5:238.
15. *Deseret Weekly* 41 (Oct. 11, 1890): 517; see also Stuy, *Collected Discourses,* 2:106.

travels in the southern country last winter I had many interviews with President Young, and with Heber C. Kimball, and Geo. A. Smith, and Jedediah M. Grant, and many others who are dead. They attended our conference, they attended our meetings."[16]

In 1896 Elder Abraham H. Cannon, a member of the Quorum of the Twelve Apostles, was unexpectedly taken in death. Only thirty-seven years old, he had served in the quorum for nearly seven years. President Wilford Woodruff was troubled by the early death of this brother, as were other leaders and members of the Church. And yet President Woodruff trusted in the Lord, saying: "There is a meaning to this. Many times things take place with us that we do not comprehend, unless it is given to us by revelation. But there is a meaning in the loss of that young apostle. I had a manifestation of that while in San Francisco recently.

"One evening, as I fell asleep, I was very much troubled with evil spirits that tried to afflict me; and while laboring to throw off these spirits and their influence, there was another spirit visited me that seemed to have power over the evil spirits, and they departed from me. Before he left me he told me not to grieve because of the departure of Abraham Hoagland Cannon; for the Lord had called him to fill another important mission in the spirit world, as a pure and holy apostle from Zion in the Rocky Mountains—a labor which would not only prove a great benefit to his father's household, but to the Church and kingdom of God on the earth. I feel to name this, because it is true."[17]

---

16. *Journal of Discourses*, 21:317–18.
17. *Discourses of Wilford Woodruff*, 292.

Chapter 16

ANGELS RESTORE PRIESTHOOD, KEYS, AND MORE

❧❧❧

*We humbly declare that angels have
returned to the earth in our day.*

ELDER NEIL L. ANDERSEN

A number of angels had significant responsibilities in the restoration of the priesthood and priesthood keys in this dispensation. Michael, who is the chief of the angels, oversaw the work
of the other angels. He had an active role in this dispensation, as
did other prominent persons, including Gabriel, Raphael, Elias,
Moses, Elijah, Peter, James, John, and John the Baptist. All of
these and others were instrumental in the restoration of authority,
powers, blessings, and much more (see D&C 128:20–21).

Why were angels required to restore the priesthood and keys?
Elder Parley P. Pratt explained: "Whenever the keys of Priesthood,
or, in other words, the keys of the science of Theology, are enjoyed by man on the earth, those thus privileged are entitled to
the ministering of angels, whose business with men on the earth,
is to restore the keys of the apostleship when lost; to ordain men

---

"What Thinks Christ of Me?" *Ensign*, May 2012, 114.

to the apostleship when there has been no apostolic succession; to commit the keys of a new dispensation."[1] Following are some of the angels who restored priesthood, rights, honors, keys, and more.

MICHAEL, GABRIEL, AND RAPHAEL

Michael is Adam, Gabriel is Noah, and Raphael may be Enoch.[2] These three angels had prominent roles in the restoration of the gospel and of priesthood keys. Doctrine and Covenants 128:21 mentions these three by name as angels who declared power, rights, honors, and more.

JOHN THE BAPTIST

John was ordained by an angel when he was only eight days old (D&C 84:28), and almost two millennia later, John was the angel who conferred the Priesthood of Aaron on Joseph Smith and Oliver Cowdery. John used these words, "Upon you my fellow servants, in the name of Messiah I confer the Priesthood of Aaron, which holds the keys of the ministering of angels, and of the gospel of repentance, and of baptism by immersion for the remission of sins; and this shall never be taken again from the earth, until the sons of Levi do offer again an offering unto the Lord in righteousness" (D&C 13:1; see also 107:20).

---

1. *Key to the Science of Theology*, 113. As have numerous other Church leaders, President Joseph Fielding Smith testified: "We know Joseph Smith is a prophet . . . that he received keys and authority from angels sent for this very purpose; and that the Lord revealed to him the doctrines of salvation." "Out of the Darkness," *Ensign*, June 1971, 4.
2. See McConkie and Ostler, *Revelations of the Restoration*, 1036.

Peter, James, and John

The Lord revealed to Joseph Smith, "And also with Peter, and James, and John, whom I have sent unto you, by whom I have sent unto you, by whom I have ordained you and confirmed you to be apostles, and especial witnesses of my name, and bear the keys of your ministry and of the same things which I revealed unto them; unto whom I have committed the keys of my kingdom, and a dispensation of the gospel for the last times" (D&C 27:12–13). On September 6, 1842, Joseph Smith wrote an epistle to the Church and asked, "And again, what do we hear?" He responded to this rhetorical question by writing that we have heard from the Lord, from Moroni, and from Michael; then he added that we have heard "the voice of Peter, James, and John in the wilderness between Harmony, Susquehanna county, and Colesville, Broome county, on the Susquehanna river, declaring themselves as possessing the keys of the kingdom, and of the dispensation of the fulness of times!" (D&C 128:20).

Moses

After a vision of the Lord given to Joseph Smith and Oliver Cowdery on April 3, 1836, in the Kirtland Temple was closed, "the heavens were again opened unto us; and Moses appeared before us, and committed unto us the keys of the gathering of Israel from the four parts of the earth, and the leading of the ten tribes from the land of the north" (D&C 110:11).

Elias

After the vision of Moses given to Joseph Smith and Oliver Cowdery in the Kirtland Temple, "Elias appeared, and committed the dispensation of the gospel of Abraham, saying that in us and our seed all generations after us should be blessed" (D&C 110:12). The LDS Bible Dictionary states that a "man called Elias apparently lived in mortality in the days of Abraham, who committed the dispensation of the gospel of Abraham to Joseph Smith and Oliver Cowdery in the Kirtland (Ohio) Temple on April 3, 1836. . . . We have no specific information about the details of his mortal life or ministry."

ELIJAH

After the vision of Elias given to Joseph Smith and Oliver Cowdery in the Kirtland Temple, "another great and glorious vision burst upon us; for Elijah the prophet, who was taken to heaven without tasting death, stood before us and said: Behold, the time has fully come, which was spoken of by the mouth of Malachi—testifying that he [Elijah] should be sent, before the great and dreadful day of the Lord come—To turn the hearts of the fathers to the children, and the children to the fathers, lest the whole earth be smitten with a curse—Therefore, the keys of this dispensation are committed into our hands; and by this ye may know that the great and dreadful day of the Lord is near, even at the doors" (D&C 110:13–16). Joseph Smith explained: "Elijah was the last prophet that held the keys of the Priesthood. . . . Why send Elijah? Because he holds the keys of the authority to administer in all the ordinances of the Priesthood."[3] Also, "the spirit,

---

3. *History of the Church*, 4:211.

power, and calling of Elijah is, that ye have power to hold the key of the revelation, ordinances, oracles, powers, and endowments of the fulness of the Melchizedek Priesthood and of the kingdom of God on the earth; and to receive, obtain, and perform all the ordinances belonging to the kingdom of God."[4]

MORONI

Moroni's visitations and ministry to Joseph Smith are well known. Elder Russell M. Nelson explained: "One specific angel held keys of responsibility for the Book of Mormon. That was the angel Moroni!"[5]

DIVERS ANGELS

Doctrine and Covenants 128:20–21 refers to the angels Michael, Gabriel, Raphael, Peter, James, John, and Moroni and then adds "and divers angels." *Divers* is an archaic English word that means "diverse" or "various." Who are these other angels that Joseph referred to? They may have been other prophets from both the Old and the New World, dispensation heads and others who held keys. President John Taylor taught that "when Joseph Smith was raised up as a Prophet of God, Mormon, Moroni, Nephi and others of the ancient Prophets who formerly lived on this Continent, and Peter and John and others who lived on the Asiatic Continent, came to him and communicated to him certain principles pertaining to the Gospel of the Son of God. Why?

---

4. *History of the Church*, 6:251.
5. "Scriptural Witnesses," *Ensign*, Nov. 2007, 45.

Because they held the keys of the various dispensations, and conferred them upon him, and he upon us. He was indebted to God; and we are indebted to God and to him for all the intelligence that we have on these subjects."[6]

6. *Journal of Discourses,* 17:374–75.

Chapter 17

ANGELS' SONG AND MUSIC

❧❧❧

*A host of angels was commissioned to sing
on the night the baby Jesus was born.*

ELDER JEFFREY R. HOLLAND

The Lord's people, including mortals, angels, and exalted souls, appreciate music and song. In the premortal existence, when God laid the earth's foundations, "the morning stars sang together, and all the sons of God shouted with joy" (Job 38:6–8). During the biblical period, worshippers used music to praise God for his greatness, mercy, and goodness, and music accompanied temple dedications and other religious ceremonies. So, too, the Saints in the last dispensation employ music and song during worship services, at home, and on other occasions. Inspired music and song has many purposes. President Brigham Young taught that "music belongs in heaven to cheer God, angel, and man. If we could hear the music there is in heaven, it would overwhelm mortal man."[1]

———

"The Ministry of Angels," *Ensign,* Nov. 2008, 29.

1. Cited in Woodruff, Journal, Jan. 2, 1854.

There is much evidence that the Lord's angels also appreciate music and song. The angel who announced the birth of Jesus to the shepherds near Bethlehem was accompanied by angels who sang praises to the Lord: "And suddenly there was with the angel a multitude of the heavenly host praising God, and saying, Glory to God in the highest, and on earth peace, good will toward men." After praising God, these angels returned to heaven (Luke 2:13–15). Elder Jeffrey R. Holland has taught that this "host of angels was commissioned to sing on the night the baby Jesus was born."[2]

Many beloved Christmas hymns in the LDS hymnbook refer to angels singing at Jesus Christ's birth. Consider, for example, the following phrases from that hymnbook:

- "And Saints and angels sing."[3]
- "Sing, choirs of angels, / Sing in exultation; / Sing, all ye citizens of heav'n above!"[4]
- "Angels we have heard on high / Sweetly singing o'er the plains . . . / Him whose birth the angels sing."[5]
- "Heav'nly hosts sing Alleluia!"[6]
- "The world in solemn stillness lay / To hear the angels sing . . . / And still their heav'nly music floats . . . / The blessed angels sing . . . / Which now the angels sing."[7]

---

2. "Ministry of Angels," 29.
3. "Joy to the World," *Hymns,* no. 201.
4. "Oh, Come, All Ye Faithful," *Hymns,* no. 202.
5. "Angels We Have Heard on High," *Hymns,* no. 203.
6. "Silent Night," *Hymns,* no. 204.
7. "It Came upon the Midnight Clear," *Hymns,* no. 207.

- "Hark! the herald angels sing. . . . / With th'angelic host proclaim."[8]
- "They heard the angels singing: . . . / The angels' song of glory."[9]
- "Of angels praising God who thus / Addressed their joyful song."[10]

That the LDS hymnbook includes a preface by the First Presidency adds merit to the words of the hymns.

Other angels, besides those who sang at Jesus's birth, sing praises to God. In the opening chapter of the Book of Mormon, for example, Lehi "saw God sitting upon his throne, surrounded with numberless concourses of angels in the attitude of singing and praising their God" (1 Nephi 1:8).

On occasion in our dispensation, angels have joined mortals in singing hymns of praise and worship. Elder James E. Talmage once told an audience of a union of singing between angels and mortals: The Lord "has set heavenly beings to watch over us. . . . Our eyes are so heavy, our ears so dull, that we see and hear only the things of earth. Could our vision be opened, we would see in this room at this very moment more worshippers than are occupying these seats; could our ears be unstopped we would hear more than our own feeble voices joining in the hymns of praise that we sing."[11]

---

8. "Hark! the Herald Angels Sing," *Hymns,* no. 209.

9. "With Wondering Awe," *Hymns,* no. 210.

10. "While Shepherds Watched Their Flocks," *Hymns,* no. 211.

11. *Millennial Star* 55 (July 10, 1893): 446; see also Stuy, *Collected Discourses,* 3:291.

Prescindia Huntington, a contemporary of the Prophet Joseph Smith, bore record that angels sang a hymn while mortal Saints were praying in the temple. She recorded: "At another fast meeting I was in the temple with my sister Zina. The whole of the congregation were on their knees, praying vocally, for such was the custom at the close of the meetings when Father Smith presided; yet there was no confusion; the voices of the congregation mingled softly together. While the congregation was thus praying, we both heard, from one corner of the room above our heads, a choir of angels singing most beautifully. They were invisible to us, but myriads of angelic voices seemed to be united in singing some song of Zion, and their sweet harmony filled the temple of God."[12]

Some individuals through the decades since the restoration of the gospel began have testified that they have seen and heard angels at the Lord's temples. Helen Mar Whitney, daughter of President Heber C. and Vilate Kimball and mother of Elder Orson F. Whitney, related: "It brought to my mind the testimony of many who were present at the dedication of the Manti Temple, whose eyes were opened, and they bore witness of many glorious visions, of personages who appeared to them with the heavenly music and singing, which was heard at different times, all proving that we are not separated from those who were co-workers with us here, and are still engaged in the interest of those with whom they labored for years in establishing the principles of this Gospel,

12. Tullidge, *Women of Mormondom,* 207–8.

and planning for the holy Temples, in which the work is continuing on for the living and for the dead."[13]

The following occurrence, recorded in the Church's *Millennial Star,* also took place at the dedication of the Manti Temple: "On the 21st of May, before the opening exercises commenced, Brother A. C. Smyth, the chorister, seated himself at the organ, and rendered a piece of sacred music, a selection from Mendelssohn, at the conclusion of which, persons sitting near the centre of the hall, and also on the stand at the west end, heard most heavenly voices and singing—it sounded to them most angelic, and appeared to be behind and above them, and they turned their heads in the direction of the sound, wondering if there was another choir in some other part of the Temple."[14]

Another witness of angelic music at the dedication of the Manti Temple was President Franklin D. Richards, who wrote: "When we dedicated the Temple at Manti, there were many brethren and sisters that saw the presence of spiritual beings, which could only be discerned by the eyes of the inner man. The Prophets Joseph, Hyrum, Brigham and various other Apostles that have gone, were seen; and not only so, but the ears of many of the faithful were touched and they heard the music of the heavenly choir that was there."[15]

---

13. "Some Serious Reflections," *Woman's Exponent* 17 (Oct. 15, 1888): 73.

14. "Spiritual Manifestations in the Manti Temple," *Millennial Star* 50 (1888): 521.

15. *Deseret Weekly* 46 (Mar. 18, 1893): 390; see also Stuy, *Collected Discourses,* 3:233. For another account of angelic music in the Manti Temple, see John D. T. McAllister, *Contributor* 16 (1894–95): 147.

Many other accounts of angelic choirs and heavenly music could be cited. There have also been instances in our dispensation when angels mingled their voices with those of mortals, perhaps not in singing but in praising God, shouting hosanna, or speaking in tongues. One such instance, recorded by Joseph Smith, occurred in January 1836. After sacred ordinances had been conducted in the house of the Lord, "the heavens were opened, and angels ministered unto us. . . . President Rigdon arose to conclude the services of the evening by invoking the blessing of heaven upon the Lord's anointed, which he did in an eloquent manner; the congregation shouted a long hosanna: the gift of tongues fell upon us in mighty power, angels mingled their voices with ours, while their presence was in our midst, and unceasing praises swelled our bosoms for the space of half-an-hour."[16]

Almost a year later, Elder Wilford Woodruff, under the date April 6, 1837, recorded the following event in the Kirtland Temple. The setting was a solemn assembly celebrating the organization of the Church seven years earlier. "I repaired to the house of the Lord at 8 o'clock A.M. . . . The First Presidency of the Church confirmed and sealed upon our heads all the blessings of the ordination, anointing and patriarchal with a seal in the presence of God and the Lamb and his holy angels. This seal was confirmed with a shout . . . Hosanna! Hosanna! Hosanna to God and the Lamb! Amen, Amen and Amen! This was repeated three times, and if ever a shout entered the portals of heaven this

16. *History of the Church*, 2:383.

did and was echoed by the angels on high and brought down the power which rested mightily upon us."[17]

When he was a young boy, President John Taylor heard angelic voices sing lovely music. According to his biographer, Elder B. H. Roberts, "young Taylor possessed a portion of the spirit of God and was very happy. Manifestations of its presence were frequent, not only in the expansion of his mind to understand doctrines and principles, but also in dreams and visions. 'Often when alone,' he writes, 'and sometimes in company, I heard sweet, soft, melodious music, as if performed by angelic or supernatural beings.'"[18]

---

17. Journal, April 6, 1837; for another example of angelic voices singing, see Woodruff, Journal, Dec. 16, 1877.
18. *Life of John Taylor*, 27–28.

Chapter 18

ANGELS DECLARE THE GOSPEL OF JESUS CHRIST

*The gospel of peace, which I have sent
mine angels to commit unto you.*

DOCTRINE & COVENANTS 27:16

The Lord calls on his servants, both mortals and angels, to declare the gospel of Jesus Christ unto the world. The servants' gospel message is one of joy because of the great gifts that our Savior has given us through his love and his atonement. The responsibility of carrying the gospel message does not belong solely to mortals, for "men and angels are to be coworkers in bringing to pass this great work," Joseph Smith explained. They "join hand in hand in bringing about this work."[1]

Before his birth, angels revealed that the Lord's name would be Jesus Christ, that he would be the Son of God, that he would be crucified, and that he would redeem those who would repent. Angels also taught about the scattering and gathering of Israel, the judgment of the "never-ending torment" that awaits the wicked,

---

1. *Teachings of the Prophet Joseph Smith*, 84, 159.

the state of the spirit world, truths regarding the "apostles of the Lamb," and much more.

ANGELS REVEAL TRUTHS ABOUT JESUS CHRIST AND HIS ATONEMENT

After Adam and Eve were driven from the Garden of Eden, the Lord commanded them to offer sacrifices. Adam obeyed, "and after many days an angel of the Lord appeared unto Adam, saying: Why dost thou offer sacrifices unto the Lord? And Adam said unto him: I know not, save the Lord commanded me. And then the angel spake, saying: This thing is a similitude of the sacrifice of the Only Begotten of the Father, which is full of grace and truth. Wherefore, thou shalt do all that thou doest in the name of the Son, and thou shalt repent and call upon God in the name of the Son forevermore" (Moses 5:6–8).

In this passage, an angel taught several truths to Adam. He taught that sacrificial offerings are symbols of Jesus Christ's atoning sacrifice, he (the angel) identified the divine names *Only Begotten* and *the Son,* and he commanded Adam to do all things in the Son's name, to repent, and to call upon God in the name of the Son. Later in this same chapter, we read of multiple angels preaching the gospel: "And thus the Gospel began to be preached, from the beginning, being declared by holy angels sent forth from the presence of God, and by his own voice, and by the gift of the Holy Ghost" (Moses 5:58).

Angels revealed various truths about Jesus Christ to Book of Mormon prophets: He "cometh, according to the words of the angel, in six hundred years from the time my father left Jerusalem" (1 Nephi 19:8); he "yieldeth himself, according to the words of the angel, as a man, into the hands of wicked men" (1 Nephi 19:10); the wicked of Jesus's day would "scourge him and crucify him, according to the words of the angel" (2 Nephi 6:9); "it must needs be expedient that Christ—for in the last night the angel spake unto me that this should be his name" (2 Nephi 10:3); and, "according to the words of the prophets, and also the word of the angel of God, his name shall be Jesus Christ, the Son of God" (2 Nephi 25:19).

Alma taught the people in the land of Ammonihah that "the Lord has sent his angel to visit many of his people, declaring unto them that they must go forth and cry mightily unto this people, saying: Repent ye. . . . And not many days hence the Son of God shall come in his glory. . . . he cometh to redeem those who will be baptized unto repentance. . . . Now behold, this is the voice of the angel, crying unto the people" (Alma 9:25–27, 29).

Moroni wrote that God "sent angels to minister unto the children of men, to make manifest concerning the coming of Christ," and also "by the ministering of angels, and by every word which proceeded forth out of the mouth of God, men began to exercise faith in Christ; and thus by faith, they did lay hold upon every good thing; and thus it was until the coming of Christ" (Moroni 7:22, 25).

An angel revealed a portion of King Benjamin's speech (see Mosiah 2:9–4:30). Benjamin told his audience: "And the things which I shall tell you are made known unto me by an angel from God. And he said unto me: Awake; and I awoke, and behold he stood before me" (Mosiah 3:2; see also vv. 3–4). The angel's role in the speech is later confirmed with these words: "When king

Benjamin had made an end of speaking the words which had been delivered unto him by the angel of the Lord" (Mosiah 4:1). Benjamin spoke again of the angel when he instructed his audience to "humble yourselves even in the depths of humility, calling on the name of the Lord daily, and standing steadfastly in the faith of that which is to come, which was spoken by the mouth of the angel" (Mosiah 4:11); his audience later referred to the same angel (see Mosiah 5:5).

ANGELS TEACH THE GOSPEL

Alma taught that angels declare the joyful news of the gospel to all nations: "Yea, and the voice of the Lord, by the mouth of angels, doth declare it unto all nations; yea, doth declare it, that they may have glad tidings of great joy; yea, and he doth sound these glad tidings among all his people, yea, even to them that are scattered abroad upon the face of the earth" (Alma 13:22). Alma added: "For behold, angels are declaring it unto many at this time in our land; and this is for the purpose of preparing the hearts of the children of men to receive [Jesus's] word at the time of his coming in his glory. And now we only wait to hear the joyful news declared unto us by the mouth of angels, of his coming" (Alma 13:24–25).

Helaman 16:14 adds this witness: "And angels did appear unto men, wise men, and did declare unto them glad tidings of great joy."

Other Book of Mormon passages indicate that angels declared the gospel message to mortals (see Alma 39:19; Helaman 13:7). The Doctrine and Covenants, too, refers to angels delivering the gospel: "The gospel of peace, which I have sent mine angels to commit unto you" (D&C 27:16); and, "O inhabitants of the earth, I have sent forth mine angel flying through the midst of heaven, having the everlasting gospel . . . who shall appear unto many that dwell on the earth" (D&C 133:36).

Angels declare repentance to mortals

One of the chief responsibilities of angels is to call on mortals to repent: "Have miracles ceased? Behold I say unto you, Nay; neither have angels ceased to minister unto the children of men. . . . And the office of their ministry is to call men unto repentance, and to fulfill and to do the work of the covenants of the Father" (Moroni 7:29–31).

Additional scriptures support the truth that angels declare repentance: "Well doth [the Lord] cry unto this people, by the voice of his angels: Repent ye, repent, for the kingdom of heaven is at hand" (Alma 10:20; see also 9:25, 29). God "hath sent his angels to declare the tidings of the conditions of repentance, which bringeth unto the power of the Redeemer, unto the salvation of their souls" (Helaman 5:11). And "I, the Lord God, gave unto Adam and unto his seed, that they should not die as to the temporal death, until I, the Lord God, should send forth angels to declare unto them repentance and redemption, through faith on the name of mine Only Begotten Son" (D&C 29:42).

The book of Mosiah features an example of an angel who declares repentance to an individual: Alma the Younger, who, together with the sons of Mosiah, was working "to destroy the church of God . . . and to lead astray the people of the Lord" (Mosiah 27:10). "As they were going about rebelling against God, behold, the angel of the Lord appeared unto them; and he descended as it were in a cloud; and he spake as it were with a voice of thunder, which caused the earth to shake upon which they stood; and so great was their astonishment, that they fell to the earth, and understood not the words which he spake unto them. Nevertheless, he cried again, saying: Alma, arise and stand forth, for why persecutest thou the church of God?" (Mosiah 27:11–13).

The angel continued, stating that Alma's father and others had prayed with great faith that Alma would come to know the truth. The angel said: "And now behold, can ye dispute the power of God? For behold, doth not my voice shake the earth? And can ye not also behold me before you? And I am sent from God" (Mosiah 27:14–15; see also Alma 36:6–10).

When individuals repent of their sins, angels experience a feeling of happiness. Jesus explained, "I say unto you, there is joy in the presence of the angels of God over one sinner that repenteth" (Luke 15:10).

Angels reveal truths about Jesus Christ and his atonement, they teach the joyful news of the gospel, and they declare repentance to mortals. Furthermore, angels have taught many other doctrines of the gospel. An angel spoke of the scattering and gathering of the house of Israel—"for thus saith the angel, . . . they shall be scattered, and smitten, . . . they shall be gathered together again to the lands of their inheritance" (2 Nephi 6:11). An angel presented truths about the world of spirits: "Behold, it has been made known unto me by an angel, that the spirits of all men, as soon as they are departed from this mortal body, yea, the spirits of all men, whether they be good or evil, are taken home to that

God who gave them life" (Alma 40:11). An angel taught regarding the Lord's apostles (1 Nephi 11:34). And angels imparted the plan of salvation: God "in his mercy he doth visit us by his angels, that the plan of salvation might be made known unto us as well as unto future generations" (Alma 24:14).

Angels likewise bear testimony of God and his Son: "Enoch beheld angels descending out of heaven, bearing testimony of the Father and Son" (Moses 7:27). Angels warn earth's inhabitants to prepare for God's judgments (D&C 88:92), and angels and mortals join forces with nature to warn the nations to repent (D&C 43:23–26). And the goal of the Three Nephites is to bring souls to Jesus Christ (3 Nephi 29:29). Thus in many ways do angels work to teach the gospel of Christ to the inhabitants of the world.

Chapter 19

ANGELS ARE MESSENGERS OF LOVE, PEACE, AND COMFORT

❧❀❧

*In our hour of deepest sorrow, we can receive
profound peace from the words of the angel that first
Easter morning: "He is not here: for he is risen."*

PRESIDENT THOMAS S. MONSON

The scriptures refer to both "ministering spirits" (JST, Hebrews 1:6–7, 14; Moroni 10:14) and "ministering of angels" (Jacob 7:17; Omni 1:25). Many scriptural characters have been the recipients of ministering spirits and angels. Nephi, the son of Lehi, for example, declared that "angels came down and ministered unto me" (2 Nephi 4:24; 1 Nephi 11:14) and Helaman's grandson Nephi had such great "faith on the Lord Jesus Christ that angels did minister unto him daily" (3 Nephi 7:18). Jesus's disciples in 3 Nephi 19, too, benefited from angels' ministering: "Angels did come down out of heaven and did minister unto them" (3 Nephi 19:14). These disciples were exceptionally blessed—"while the angels were ministering unto the disciples, behold, Jesus came and stood in the midst and ministered

---

"He Is Risen!" *Ensign,* May 2010, 90.

unto them" (3 Nephi 19:15). Other recipients of angelic ministering in the Book of Mormon include King Benjamin (Mosiah 3:2), Alma the Younger (Mosiah 27:10–11; Alma 8:14), Amulek (Alma 10:7), Samuel the Lamanite (Helaman 13:7), and others. The Old and New Testaments also present many accounts of angels ministering to people.

And in our own dispensation, the ministering of angels has not ceased. President Thomas S. Monson cited President Joseph F. Smith's testimony that "authority that has been given in this day in which we live by ministering angels and spirits from above, *direct from the presence of Almighty God.*"[1] In addition, President Boyd K. Packer declared, "The promptings of the Spirit, the dreams, and the visions and the visitations, and the ministering of angels all are with us now."[2]

President Boyd K. Packer, on another occasion, stated in no uncertain terms that "angels attend the rank and file of the Church." He then provided examples of how angels minister to Church members: "Who would dare to say that angels do not now attend the rank and file of the Church who—answer the calls to the mission fields, teach the classes, pay their tithes and offerings, seek for the records of their forebears, work in the temples, raise their children in faith, and have brought this work through 150 years?"[3]

---

1. *Gospel Doctrine,* 139–40; italics added; cited in Monson, "Willing and Worthy to Serve," *Ensign,* May 2012, 66.
2. "Revelation in a Changing World," *Ensign,* Nov. 1989, 16.
3. *Mine Errand from the Lord,* 385.

ANGELS MINISTER WITH HEAVENLY LOVE

All angels minister with heavenly love, and every angelic communication to the Saints is a message of love. Oliver Cowdery personally experienced the love of John the Baptist when John appeared to him and Joseph Smith. Sometime after John's visitation, Oliver wrote that this angel's "love [was] enkindled upon our souls."[4]

Decades later, President Joseph F. Smith, in the April 1916 general conference, spoke of the love of heavenly messengers: "I believe we move and have our being in the presence of heavenly messengers and of heavenly beings. We are not separated from them. . . . I claim that we live in their presence, they see us, they are solicitous for our welfare, they love us now more than ever. . . . [T]heir love for us and their desire for our well being must be greater than that which we feel for ourselves."[5]

We lack specific knowledge of what President Smith meant when he spoke of *heavenly messengers* and *beings.* Did he refer to resurrected beings? Translated beings? Some other beings? Regardless, President Joseph F. Smith explained that deceased loved ones—ministering spirits—may bring messages of love. He specifically mentioned fathers, mothers, brothers, sisters, and also friends who were faithful and taught that they "may have a mission given them to visit their relatives and friends upon the earth again, bringing . . . messages of love."[6] More recently, Elder Jeffrey R. Holland witnessed that "from the beginning down

---

4. Cited in Roberts, *Comprehensive History,* 1:178.
5. Conference Report, Apr. 1916, 2–3.
6. *Gospel Doctrine,* 436.

through the dispensations, God has used angels as His emissaries in conveying love and concern for His children."[7]

Elder Parley P. Pratt gave us an account of a ministering spirit communicating love to a mortal. At one point in his life, Elder Pratt was held captive for months in a Missouri dungeon. He was very discouraged. After fasting and praying for a number of days, he experienced a powerful answer to his prayer: "A personage . . . stood before me with a smile of compassion in every look, and pity mingled with the tenderest love and sympathy in every expression of the countenance. . . . A well-known voice saluted me, which I readily recognized as that of the wife of my youth, who had for nearly two years been sweetly sleeping where the weary are at rest."[8] This personage, as an angelic messenger, delivered her message to Parley and then departed.

ANGELS CALM TROUBLED HEARTS

Angels' assignments may be "very grand and have significance for the whole world," but more often, their assignments are private and personal, explained Elder Jeffrey R. Holland. Although angels have various sacred goals and purposes, time and again their chief assignment is to provide comfort to a suffering or grieving mortal. Elder Holland taught: "Occasionally the angelic purpose is to warn. But most often it is to comfort, to provide some form of merciful attention, guidance in difficult times."[9]

---

7. "The Ministry of Angels," *Ensign*, Nov. 2008, 29.
8. *Autobiography of Parley P. Pratt*, 261–62.
9. "Ministry of Angels," 29.

On another occasion, Elder Holland elaborated: "When we weep [God] and the angels of heaven weep with us."[10]

We have scriptural record of angels who have ministered to those in need of comfort. During his ministry as a missionary and apostle, Paul experienced many extreme trials: His enemies severely whipped him on five different occasions—on each occasion, he was lashed 39 times; on another occasion he was stoned; three different times he was on a ship that was shipwrecked (once he remained in the waters of the sea for a day and a night); and on three different occasions those who opposed him beat him with rods (see 2 Corinthians 11:24–25). In addition to these extreme trials, Paul was falsely imprisoned, bitten by a poisonous snake, and subjected to many more tribulations. At some point during these trials, Abel, as a ministering angel, appeared to Paul and comforted him. Abel had "become an angel of God by receiving his body from the dead, holding still the keys of his dispensation; and was sent down from heaven unto Paul to minister consoling words, and to commit unto him a knowledge of the mysteries of godliness."[11]

Another ministering angel who calmed troubled hearts is spoken of in Matthew's Gospel. On the morning of Jesus Christ's resurrection, two women named Mary drew near to the tomb where Jesus's body had been buried. There they beheld an angel, who declared, "He is not here: for he is risen" (Matthew 28:6). After citing these words of the angel, President Thomas S.

---

10. "Lessons from Liberty Jail," *Ensign*, Sept. 2009, 29.
11. *Teachings of the Prophet Joseph Smith*, 169.

Monson testified, "No words in Christendom mean more to me than those spoken by the angel to the weeping Mary Magdalene and the other Mary." President Monson likened this account of the angel speaking to the two women to us: "My beloved brothers and sisters, in our hour of deepest sorrow, we can receive profound peace from the words of the angel that first Easter morning."[12]

Yet another scriptural example of an angel who comforts a mortal is the angel who visited Alma. He was "weighed down with sorrow, wading through much tribulation and anguish of soul" because of the great iniquities of the people of Ammonihah. At that point, Alma needed great comfort from a higher source. As he was traveling, "behold an angel of the Lord appeared unto him, saying: Blessed art thou, Alma; therefore, lift up thy head and rejoice, for thou hast great cause to rejoice" (Alma 8:14–15). This angel turned the deep emotions of sorrow and anguish of soul to rejoicing.

Alma's experience was not unique to God's prophets or to individuals we read about in scripture. Elder Jeffrey R. Holland assured us that "Christ and His angels and His prophets forever labor to buoy up our spirits, steady our nerves, calm our hearts, send us forth with renewed strength and resolute hope. They wish all to know that 'if God be for us, who can be against us?' In the

---

12. "He Is Risen!" *Ensign*, May 2010, 90. President Gordon B. Hinckley, too, found great peace in the same words of the angel: "In the hour of deepest sorrow we draw hope and peace and certitude from the words of the angel that Easter morning, 'He is not here: for he is risen, as he said' (Matthew 28:6)." "This Glorious Easter Morn," *Ensign*, May 1996, 67.

world we shall have tribulation, but we are to be of good cheer."[13] President Dieter F. Uchtdorf witnessed that angels may attend those who experience great sorrow: "There are those among you who, although young, have already suffered a full measure of grief and sorrow. My heart is filled with compassion and love for you. How dear you are to the Church. How beloved you are of your Heavenly Father. Though it may seem that you are alone, angels attend you."[14]

President Harold B. Lee related the tragic experience of John Wells, a member of the Presiding Bishopric, and his wife, Almena, when their son was killed by a freight train in a canyon near Salt Lake City, Utah. Both parents experienced deep sorrow and heartache, but President Lee explained, "Sister Wells was inconsolable." Her mourning and grieving, which began when she first heard of the accident and continued through the funeral, did not seem to help. She was "in a rather serious state of mind." Soon after the funeral, while Sister Wells was mourning on her bed, "her son appeared to her and said, 'Mother do not mourn, do not cry. I am all right.'" Her son explained the nature of the accident, that he had tripped on a root and fell on the tracks as the train passed. "He said that as soon as he realized that he was in another environment he tried to see his father, but couldn't reach him. His father was so busy with the duties in his office he could not respond to his call. Therefore he had come to his mother. He said to her, 'You tell Father that all is well with me,

---

13. "The Peaceable Things of the Kingdom," *Ensign,* Nov. 1996, 83.
14. "Your Happily Ever After," *Ensign,* May 2010, 126.

and I want you not to mourn any more.'"[15] Bishop and Sister Wells's son had appeared as a ministering spirit to comfort his parents after his untimely death.

Another account of a spirit who ministered comfort to a mortal was published in the *Relief Society Magazine.* This story related an experience of a young woman who in 1915 attended the Salt Lake Temple to be married. This young woman's mother had passed away some years earlier, so her grandmother and others accompanied her to the temple. The article related that "just as the final blessing was pronounced upon the young couple, the young girl raised her hand and spoke the name of her mother. 'There's my mother, don't you see her? can't you see her? Oh, my mother!' cried the weeping bride who melted with exquisite sorrow at the vision of her noble mother.

"So profound was the impression, so pure was the manifestation, that nearly everyone present in the room wept in sympathy with this lovely and blessed bride."[16]

Zera Pulsipher, who was born in 1789 and died in 1872, lost his beloved wife when he was about twenty-two years of age. She left behind their little girl named Harriett. For some time, Zera remained anxious about his wife's "state and condition" in the world of spirits, and consequently, he wrote, "She came to me in vision and appearing natural looked pleasant as she ever did and sat by my side and assisted me in singing a hymn—beginning thus: 'That glorious day is drawing nigh when Zions Light Shall

---

15. *Teachings of Harold B. Lee,* 415.
16. "A Friend of the Helpless Dead," *Relief Society Magazine* 4 (Sept. 1917): 486.

Shine.' This she did with a seeming composure. This vision took away all the anxiety of my mind concerning her in as much as she seemed to enjoy herself well. . . . My mind became calm as respecting her condition in the spirit world."[17]

President Wilford Woodruff told a large group of Saints of a dream that he had received from the Lord, which dream prepared him for the death of his first child. At the time, Wilford was serving as a missionary far from home, in London, England, together with Elder George A. Smith. In this dream Wilford's wife visited him and informed him that their child had passed away. He recognized that the dream was inspired, and the next morning at breakfast, with great sadness Wilford told his companion of his dream. The following morning Wilford received a letter from his wife, "conveying the intelligence of the death of my child." He testified that the dream had served "to prepare my mind for the news of the death of my child. . . . My dream gave me a strong testimony of the resurrection. I am satisfied, always have been, in regard to the resurrection. I rejoice in it. The way was opened unto us by the blood of the Son of God."[18]

---

17. "History of Zera Pulsipher," 5.
18. *Journal of Discourses*, 22:333.

Chapter 20

"MINE ANGELS ROUND ABOUT YOU, TO BEAR YOU UP"

There are both true servants and angels to help you along the lighted path.

PRESIDENT HENRY B. EYRING

Elder Jeffrey R. Holland indicated that one of President Thomas S. Monson's favorite scriptures is Doctrine and Covenants 84:88: "I will go before your face. I will be on your right hand and on your left, and my Spirit shall be in your hearts, and mine angels round about you, to bear you up."[1] President Monson has cited this verse in a number of his talks and sermons. For example, he has taught: "You are entitled to His divine help, for He has promised you: 'I will go before your face. I will be on your right hand and on your left, and my Spirit shall be in your hearts, and mine angels round about you, to bear you up.'"[2]

Doctrine and Covenants 84:88 uses military language, where an army marching to war or a convoy traveling to battle has an

---

"Walk in the Light," *Ensign,* May 2008, 125.

1. "The Ministry of Angels," *Ensign,* Nov. 2008, 31.
2. "Bring Him Home," *Ensign,* Nov. 2003, 58.

advance and a rear guard as well as soldiers protecting the right and left flanks from enemy combatants. In verse 88, Jesus Christ himself is our advance guard ("I will go before your face") as well as our protector for both our right and left flanks ("I will be on your right hand and on your left"). Moreover, the Lord's angels surround us ("and mine angels round about you") to bear us up. "To bear up" may mean "to minister" or to attend to one's needs.

ANGELS WHO MINISTERED IN 1836

During the Kirtland period of Latter-day Saint history, especially during the first half of 1836, a number of holy angels appeared unto many Saints and ministered to them. Joseph Smith recorded: "Many . . . saw glorious visions also. Angels ministered unto them, as well as to myself, and the power of the Highest rested upon us, the house was filled with the glory of God, and we shouted Hosanna to God and the Lamb."[3] "The visions of heaven was opened to them . . . others were ministered unto by holy angels, and the spirit of prophecy and revelation was poured out in mighty power; and loud hosannas, and glory to God in the highest, saluted the heavens, for we all communed with the heavenly host."[4] And again, Joseph Smith wrote: "President Frederick G. Williams arose and testified that while President Rigdon was making his first prayer, an angel entered the window and took his seat between Father Smith and himself, and

---

3. *History of the Church,* 2:381.
4. *History of the Church,* 2:382.

remained there during the prayer. President David Whitmer also saw angels in the house."[5]

The Prophet recorded that "a noise was heard like the sound of a rushing mighty wind, which filled the Temple, and all the congregation simultaneously arose, being moved upon by an invisible power; many began to speak in tongues and prophesy; others saw glorious visions; and I beheld the Temple was filled with angels, which fact I declared to the congregation. The people of the neighborhood came running together (hearing an unusual sound within, and seeing a bright light like a pillar of fire resting upon the Temple), and were astonished at what was taking place."[6]

Joseph recorded further, "Angels ministered to [many present], and it was a Pentecost and an endowment indeed, long to be remembered."[7]

Others in addition to Joseph Smith have testified that angels appeared and ministered in the Kirtland Temple. President Wilford Woodruff wrote: "I repaired to the house of the Lord at an early hour in the morning to spend the day in prayer and fasting with the saints in Kirtland, as this was a day set apart for that purpose. . . . The power of God rested upon the people. The gifts were poured out upon us. Some had the administering of angels & the image of God sat upon the countenances of the Saints."[8] According to Elder George A. Smith, "on the evening

---

5. *History of the Church*, 2:427; see also the account of William Draper, cited in Dieter F. Uchtdorf, "Hold on a Little Longer," *Ensign*, Jan. 2010, 6.

6. *History of the Church*, 2:428.

7. *History of the Church*, 2:432–33.

8. Journal, Mar. 23, 1837.

after the dedication of the Temple, hundreds of the brethren received the ministering of angels, saw the light and personages of angels, and bore testimony of it. They spake in new tongues, and had a greater manifestation of the power of God than that described by Luke on the day of Pentecost."[9] Elder Smith wrote further, "Many individuals bore testimony that they saw angels, and David Whitmer bore testimony that he saw three angels passing up the south aisle, and there came a shock on the house like the sound of a mighty rushing wind, and almost every man in the house arose, and hundreds of them were speaking in tongues, prophesying or declaring visions, almost with one voice."[10]

Stephen Post likewise recorded events at the Kirtland Temple dedication, on March 28, 1836: "This eve the Spirit of the Lord rested on the congregation many spake in tongues many prophesied, angels were in our midst, & ministered unto some. Cloven tongues like unto fire rested upon those who spake in tongues & prophesied when they ceased to speak the tongues ascended." In a letter to his wife, Sally Phelps, written sometime between April 1 and 6, 1836, William W. Phelps recounted that an "angel came in on the first seat during the prayer."[11]

Angels may minister to us for a myriad of purposes, according to our temporal and spiritual needs, always in keeping with the Lord's divine will. The following examples are representative of how angels may minister to us.

---

9. *Journal of Discourses,* 2:215.

10. *Journal of Discourses,* 11:10.

11. Harper, "Pentecost and Endowment Indeed," in Welch and Carlson, *Opening the Heavens,* 352, 347.

Angels may help individuals overcome addictions

In 2010 two members of the Quorum of the Twelve Apostles directed counsel to individuals who wrestle with addictions of various kinds. Both of those conference addresses indicate that angels are available to render divine assistance to individuals with addictions who desire to forsake them. First, in the April general conference, Elder Jeffrey R. Holland provided these inspired instructions: "Acknowledge that people bound by the chains of true addictions often need more help than self-help, and that may include you. Seek that help and welcome it. Talk to your bishop. Follow his counsel. Ask for a priesthood blessing. Use the Church's Family Services offerings or seek other suitable professional help. Pray without ceasing. Ask for angels to help you. . . .

"Cultivate and be where the Spirit of the Lord is. Make sure that includes your own home or apartment, dictating the kind of art, music, and literature you keep there. If you are endowed, go to the temple as often as your circumstances allow. Remember that the temple arms you 'with [God's] power, . . . [puts His] glory . . . round about [you], and [gives His] angels . . . charge over [you].'"[12]

Later that same year, in the October general conference, President Boyd K. Packer taught: "The twin principles of repentance and forgiveness exceed in strength the awesome power of the tempter. If you are bound by a habit or an addiction that is unworthy, you must stop conduct that is harmful. Angels will

---

12. "Place No More for the Enemy of My Soul," *Ensign,* May 2010, 45–46.

coach you, and priesthood leaders will guide you through those difficult times."[13]

Angels may inspire confidence

While serving as a young missionary, President Joseph F. Smith received a vision that gave him great confidence. In the vision, he wrote, "I was hurrying as fast as I could. . . . I turned aside quickly and went into the bath and washed myself clean. I opened up this little bundle that I had, and there was a pair of white, clean garments. . . . I put them on. Then I rushed to what appeared to be a great opening, or door. I knocked and the door opened, and the man who stood there was the Prophet Joseph Smith. He looked at me a little reprovingly, and the first words he said: 'Joseph, you are late.' Yet I took confidence and said:

"'Yes, but I am clean—I am clean!'

"He clasped my hand and drew me in, then closed the great door." When Joseph F. Smith entered through the door, he saw his father and his mother, Brigham Young, Heber C. Kimball, Willard Richards, and "a vast multitude of people . . . who seemed to be among the chosen, among the exalted."

President Smith recalled: "When I awoke that morning I was a man, although only a boy. There was not anything in the world that I feared. I could meet any man or woman or child and look them in the face, feeling in my soul that I was a man every whit. That vision, that manifestation and witness that I enjoyed at that time made me what I am, if I am anything that is good, or clean,

13. "Cleansing the Inner Vessel," *Ensign*, Nov. 2010, 76.

or upright before the Lord, if there is anything good in me. That has helped me out in every trial and through every difficulty."

Joseph's experience was not merely a dream but so real and full of meaning that he wrote, "To me it is a reality. . . . I know that that was a reality, to show me my duty."[14]

Just as President Joseph F. Smith was shown duty in a vision, so President Wilford Woodruff, when he was in his "boyhood," was visited by an angel who revealed many things to him. President Woodruff later stated that this personage "was doubtless sent to me for the purpose of strengthening me and giving me encouragement in my labors."[15]

Angels May Prompt One to Serve the Lord

Elder Parley P. Pratt was working on his farm when an angel called him to serve the Lord. Parley had plowed about six acres to prepare the ground for wheat, and he had been cutting and splitting logs to make fence posts. One night he had a dream, or a "night vision." In this dream, a man approached him and called out, "'Parley, Parley. . . . Cease splitting rails, for the Lord has prepared you for a greater work.'" Parley wanted evidence that the dream was inspired, so he asked the messenger, "'Whereby shall I know that this message is from the Lord?'"[16] The messenger gave Parley the required evidence, and he soon thereafter left his temporal work. As history attests, Elder Parley P. Pratt later

14. *Life of Joseph F. Smith,* 445–47.
15. *Deseret Weekly* 53 (Nov. 7, 1896): 642.
16. *Autobiography of Parley P. Pratt,* 98.

became a powerful missionary, a great servant of the Lord in this dispensation.

Angels May Help During Trials and Severe Hardships

Many individuals in mortality have experienced extreme hardships, such as those experienced by Latter-day Saint pioneers who suffered severe privation as they crossed oceans and plains to journey to Zion. Angels, at times, bore up such individuals. The following story recounted by President David O. McKay serves as a case in point of angels who assisted mortals in times of great need. President McKay cited the testimony of Francis Webster, a member of the Martin handcart company: "I was in that company and my wife was in it. . . . We suffered beyond anything you can imagine and many died of exposure and starvation. . . .

"I have pulled my handcart when I was so weak and weary from illness and lack of food that I could hardly put one foot ahead of the other. I have looked ahead and seen a patch of sand or a hill slope and I have said, I can go only that far and there I must give up, for I cannot pull the load through it. . . . I have gone on to that sand and when I reached it, the cart began pushing me. I have looked back many times to see who was pushing my cart, but my eyes saw no one. I knew then that the angels of God were there."[17]

President Harold B. Lee explained that even Jesus Christ in his extremity had need of ministering angels: "Sometimes when you are going through the most severe tests, you will be nearer

---

17. "Pioneer Women," *Relief Society Magazine* 35, no. 1 (Jan. 1948): 8; see also Olsen, *Price We Paid*, 2–3.

to God than you have any idea, for like the experience of the Master Himself in the temptation on the mount, in the Garden of Gethsemane, and on the cross at Calvary, the scriptures record, 'And, behold, angels came and ministered unto him' (Matthew 4:11). Sometimes that may happen to you in the midst of your trials."[18]

Angels may provide other kinds of temporal assistance

Angels have provided other kinds of temporal assistance to mortals. For example, in scripture we read that an angel provided food and water to the prophet Elijah when he fled for his life from Jezebel (1 Kings 19:1–7). In our own dispensation, President Heber C. Kimball spoke of a time when he and Brigham Young traveled together in doing the Lord's work. They had only $13.50 between them, but along the way they paid for travel, lodgings, and meals. In fact, they paid out more than $87. President Kimball observed: "Brother Brigham often suspected that I put the money in his trunk or clothes, thinking I had . . . money which I had not acquainted him with, but this was not so. The money could only have been put in his trunk by some heavenly messenger who administered to our necessities daily, as he knew we needed."[19]

President Wilford Woodruff and President Young were conversing about various topics when "the subject of miracles came up." President Young told Wilford, "I have had a $5 gold piece

---

18. *Teachings of Harold B. Lee,* 192.
19. "One York Shilling," in *Best-Loved Stories,* 375.

put into my pocket now two days in succession. I do not know from what source it came from. Brother Kimball said it was an angel."[20]

Angels may appear in answer to a prayer

We know that angels on occasion respond to heartfelt prayers, according to the Lord's will. For example, when rebellious Alma the Younger was "seeking to destroy the church" an angel appeared to him (Alma 36:6). How can an angel appear to a wicked man? President Boyd K. Packer explained that Alma "was struck down by an angel, not because he deserved it but because of the prayers of his father and others (see Mosiah 27:14)."[21]

Angels may assist in healing the sick

President Harold B. Lee's experience on an airplane illustrates the truth that angels may participate in healing a mortal who has an illness. President Lee recalled: "I was suffering from an ulcer condition that was becoming worse and worse. We had been touring a mission; my wife, Joan, and I were impressed the next morning that we should get home as quickly as possible, although we had planned to stay for some other meetings.

"On the way across the country, we were sitting in the forward section of the airplane. Some of our Church members were in the next section. As we approached a certain point en route, someone laid his hand upon my head. I looked up; I could see no one. That happened again before we arrived home, again with the same experience. Who it was, by what means or what medium,

---

20. Journal, Nov. 13, 1856.
21. "I Will Remember Your Sins No More," *Ensign*, May 2006, 26.

I may never know, except I knew that I was receiving a blessing that I came a few hours later to know I needed most desperately.

" . . . shortly [after we reached home], there came massive hemorrhages which, had they occurred while we were in flight, I wouldn't be here today talking about it.

"I know that there are powers divine that reach out when all other help is not available. . . . Yes, I know that there are such powers."[22]

President Brigham Young testified: "Supposing we were traveling in the mountains, and all we had or could get, in the shape of nourishment, was a little venison, and one or two were taken sick, without anything in the world in the shape of healing medicine within our reach, what should we do? According to my faith, ask the Lord Almighty to send an angel to heal the sick. This is our privilege, when so situated that we cannot get anything to help ourselves."[23]

Other individuals have related that angels were instrumental in healing their respective sicknesses, including John R. Young, a young man serving a mission in Hawaii; Mary Elizabeth Rollins Lightner, a woman who lived during the Nauvoo period of the Church; Orin Alonzo Perry, who in the fall of 1893 was near the point of death; and a young English girl who had a severe fever.[24]

---

22. "Stand Ye in Holy Places," *Ensign,* July 1973, 123; see also *Best-Loved Stories,* 1:325–26.

23. *Journal of Discourses,* 4:25. Elder Parley P. Pratt set forth a variety of occasions in which one would wish for a ministering angel, including this one: "Why, if a person is sick they would like to be visited, comforted, or healed by an angel or spirit!" *Journal of Discourses,* 1:13.

24. Young, *Memoirs of John R. Young,* 76–77; Adam, "Mary Elizabeth Rollins

President James E. Faust summarized the ministering of angels: "In ancient and modern times angels have appeared and given instruction, warnings, and direction, which benefited the people they visited. We do not consciously realize the extent to which ministering angels affect our lives. President Joseph F. Smith said, 'In like manner our fathers and mothers, brothers, sisters and friends who have passed away from this earth, having been faithful, and worthy to enjoy these rights and privileges, may have a mission given them to visit their relatives and friends upon the earth again, bringing from the divine Presence messages of love, of warning, or reproof and instruction, to those whom they had learned to love in the flesh.' Many of us feel that we have had this experience. Their ministry has been and is an important part of the gospel."[25]

Lightner, 1818–1913," 16–18; "Orin Alonzo Perry," in Whitney, *History of Utah*, 4:440; "Nellie Colebrook," *Young Woman's Journal* 2 (Apr. 1891): 292–93.

25. "A Royal Priesthood," *Ensign*, May 2006, 51.

Chapter 21

ANGELS ANNOUNCE CHILDREN YET TO BE BORN

※※※ ※※※

The angel said unto [Mary] . . . thou
shalt conceive in thy womb, and bring forth
a son, and shalt call his name Jesus.

LUKE 1:30–31

The Bible records narratives wherein an angel announces the forthcoming birth of a child. Angels announced forthcoming children to Hagar, the mother of Ishmael (Genesis 16:7–11); Manoah's wife, the mother of Samson (Judges 13:3–21); Zacharias, the father of John the Baptist (Luke 1:11–19); and Mary, the mother of Jesus (Luke 1:26–38). The following verses are selected from each of these narratives.

HAGAR, MOTHER OF ISHMAEL

"And the angel of the Lord said unto her, I will multiply thy seed exceedingly, that it shall not be numbered for multitude. And the angel of the Lord said unto her, Behold, thou art with child, and shalt bear a son, and shalt call his name Ishmael; because the Lord hath heard thy affliction" (Genesis 16:10–11).

MANOAH'S WIFE, MOTHER OF SAMSON

"And the angel of the Lord appeared unto the woman, and said unto her, Behold now, thou art barren, and bearest not: but thou shalt conceive, and bear a son. . . . Then the woman came and told her husband, saying, A man of God came unto me, and his countenance was like the countenance of an angel of God, very terrible: but I asked him not whence he was, neither told he me his name. . . . So Manoah took a kid with a meat offering, and offered it upon a rock unto the Lord: and the angel did wondrously; and Manoah and his wife looked on. For it came to pass, when the flame went up toward heaven from off the altar, that the angel of the Lord ascended in the flame of the altar. And Manoah and his wife looked on it, and fell on their faces to the ground. But the angel of the Lord did no more appear to Manoah and to his wife. Then Manoah knew that he was an angel of the Lord" (Judges 13:3–21).

ZACHARIAS, FATHER OF JOHN THE BAPTIST

"And there appeared unto him an angel of the Lord standing on the right side of the altar of incense. . . . But the angel said unto him, Fear not, Zacharias: for thy prayer is heard; and thy wife Elisabeth shall bear thee a son, and thou shalt call his name John. . . . And Zacharias said unto the angel, Whereby shall I know this? for I am an old man, and my wife well stricken in years. And the angel answering said unto him, I am Gabriel, that stand in the presence of God; and am sent to speak unto thee, and to shew thee these glad tidings" (Luke 1:11–19).

MARY, THE MOTHER OF JESUS

"And in the sixth month the angel Gabriel was sent from God unto a city of Galilee, named Nazareth. . . . And the angel came in unto her, and said, Hail, thou that art highly favoured, the Lord is with thee: blessed art thou among women. . . . And the angel said unto her, Fear not, Mary: for thou hast found favour with God. And, behold, thou shalt conceive in thy womb, and bring forth a son, and shalt call his name JESUS. . . . Then said Mary unto the angel, How shall this be, seeing I know not a man? And the angel answered and said unto her, The Holy Ghost shall come upon thee, and the power of the Highest shall overshadow thee: therefore also that holy thing which shall be born of thee shall be called the Son of God. . . . And Mary said, Behold the handmaid of the Lord; be it unto me according to thy word. And the angel departed from her" (Luke 1:26–38).

The four narratives share common themes:

1. Each explicitly states that the angel is from the Lord ("the angel of the Lord").

2. The angel appeared to each individual; these visitations were very real visitations from heavenly messengers.

3. The angel spoke to the individual: Hagar, "And the angel of the Lord said unto her"; Manoah's wife, "And the angel of the Lord appeared unto the woman, and said unto her"; Zacharias, "the angel said unto him"; and Mary, "the angel came in unto her, and said."

4. The angel stated that a child would be born: Hagar, "Behold, thou art with child, and shalt bear a son"; Manoah's wife, "thou shalt conceive, and bear a son"; Zacharias, "thy wife

Elisabeth shall bear thee a son"; Mary, "thou shalt conceive in thy womb, and bring forth a son."

5. The angel gave the name of the forthcoming child, except in the case of Manoah's wife: Hagar, "call his name Ishmael"; Manoah's wife (no name given); Zacharias, "call his name John"; and Mary, "call his name JESUS."

There are also are several differences among the narratives. For example, in three of the narratives, the angel appears to the mothers-to-be, but in the other narrative, the angel appears to the father-to-be. The text does not explain why the angel appeared to Zacharias instead of to his wife, Elisabeth; it is possible, of course, that the angel did appear to Elisabeth but that the record of that account is no longer extant. Another difference pertains to the names of the angels. In the case of Hagar and Manoah's wife, the angels are unnamed, but in the case of Zacharias and Mary, the angel was identified as Gabriel. The angel told Zacharias, "I am Gabriel, that stand in the presence of God" (Luke 1:19). Luke wrote: "The angel Gabriel was sent from God unto a city of Galilee, named Nazareth. To a virgin . . . and the virgin's name was Mary" (Luke 1:26–27). Gabriel is none other than Noah of the Old Testament.[1]

---

1. *Teachings of the Prophet Joseph Smith*, 157.

Chapter 22

GOD'S DESTROYING ANGELS

❧✦❧

I, the Lord, give unto them a promise, that
the destroying angel shall pass by them.

DOCTRINE & COVENANTS 89:21

From time to time, in the face of wickedness, the Lord dispatches an angel to destroy one or more persons. In fact, both the scriptures and modern prophets use the expression "destroying angel." During the lifetime of Moses and Aaron, an angel destroyed the firstborn in Egypt (Exodus 12:11–12, 29), but the Lord prepared a way for his people to receive protection from this destroying angel (see Exodus 12:21–23). On the night of the first Passover, Israelites ensured that the destroying angel would pass over them by placing the blood of the Passover lamb on their doorposts before the destruction of the firstborn of Egypt. The blood of the lamb, signifying the blood of Jesus Christ, protected the children of Israel from the destroying angel.

A passage in the Doctrine and Covenants refers to the destroying angel of Exodus 12. After revealing the Word of Wisdom to Joseph Smith, the Lord made a promise to those who would obey this commandment: "And I, the Lord, give unto them a promise, that the destroying angel shall pass by them, as the children of Israel, and not slay them. Amen" (D&C 89:21).

How may we avoid the destroying angel? Elder Dallin H. Oaks taught: "Among many blessings I have received from gospel teachings are those promised for keeping the Word of Wisdom. For me these have included health and knowledge and the capacity to 'run and not be weary, and . . . walk and not faint,' and the fulfillment of the promise that 'the destroying angel shall pass by them, as the children of Israel, and not slay them' (D&C 89:18–21)."[1]

A second example in the Old Testament of a destroying angel is in the account of King David's commission of certain sins (see 1 Chronicles 21:1–30). A third example is in the account of the reign of King Hezekiah, when the Assyrian army was advancing toward Jerusalem with the intent of conquering the city. With thousands of enemy soldiers camped outside of Jerusalem's gates, waiting to destroy the city's inhabitants, Hezekiah petitioned the Lord through prayer in the temple. In response to Hezekiah's humble prayer, the Lord sent his prophet Isaiah to the king to promise deliverance from the Assyrians. Isaiah assured Hezekiah that Jerusalem's inhabitants need not fear, for the Lord would not permit the Assyrians to enter the city (see Isaiah 37:34). The Lord heard Hezekiah's prayer and sent an angel, who destroyed 185,000 soldiers in the Assyrian camp, thus saving Hezekiah and his people from destruction (see Isaiah 37:36).

The New Testament likewise contains examples of destroying

1. "The Gospel in Our Lives," *Ensign*, May 2002, 34.

angels. Acts 12 refers to an angel that destroyed an infamous ruler. The narrative relates that Herod Agrippa I, a member of the notorious Herodian family, had already "killed James the brother of John with the sword" (Acts 12:2). Because this wicked act made Herod popular among the people, he apprehended and imprisoned Peter, presumably with the intent of slaying him after Easter. Through the faith and prayers of Peter and other Church members, however, an angel helped Peter to escape from prison. Sometime after Peter's miraculous escape, Herod himself was slain by the Lord's angel. The narrative states: "And upon a set day Herod, arrayed in royal apparel, sat upon his throne, and made an oration unto them. And the people gave a shout, saying, It is the voice of a god, and not of a man. And immediately the angel of the Lord smote him, because he gave not God the glory: and he was eaten of worms, and gave up the ghost" (Acts 12:21–23).

FOUR DESTROYING ANGELS IN THE LAST DAYS

In his vision, John the Revelator saw "four angels standing on the four corners of the earth, holding the four winds of the earth, that the wind should not blow on the earth, nor on the sea, nor on any tree" (Revelation 7:1). These are God's angels who will hold great power and authority in the last days. The symbolic language of the book of Revelation shows the angels' great power: "Standing on the four corners of the earth" shows ascendancy or control (see Revelation 10:2, 5). "Four corners of the earth" means the entire earth. "Holding the four winds of the earth" indicates that the four angels have power over the winds, or the elements, of the earth. Elsewhere in the book of Revelation, angels are described as having control over fire (the angel "which had power over fire"; Revelation 14:18) and water ("the angel of the waters"; Revelation 16:5).

Joseph Smith taught many things regarding these four angels. He explained that the four angels of Revelation 7:1 are "four destroying angels holding power over the four quarters of the earth."[2] They are "sent forth from God, to whom is given power over the four parts of the earth, to save life and to destroy; these are they who have the everlasting gospel to commit to every nation, kindred, tongue, and people; having power to shut up the heavens, to seal up unto life, or to cast down to the regions of darkness" (D&C 77:8). The Prophet also explained, "The servants of God will not have gone over the nations of the Gentiles, with a warning voice, until the destroying angel will commence to waste the inhabitants of the earth, and as the prophet hath said, 'It shall be a vexation to hear the report.'"[3] Moreover, "four destroying angels holding power over the four quarters of the earth until the servants of God are sealed in their foreheads, which signifies sealing the blessing upon their heads, meaning the everlasting covenant, thereby making their calling and election sure."[4]

On another occasion, the Prophet Joseph revealed the power of temples and temple work in connection with destroying angels. He specifically referred to sealing families together in preparation for the time when the four destroying angels would be loosed: "I would advise all the Saints to go to with their might and gather

---

2. *Teachings of the Prophet Joseph Smith*, 321.
3. *Teachings of the Prophet Joseph Smith*, 87.
4. *Teachings of the Prophet Joseph Smith*, 321.

together all their living relatives to this place [the temple] that they may be sealed and saved that they may be prepared against the day that the destroying angel goes forth and if the whole Church should go to with all their might to save their dead seal their posterity and gather their living friends and spend none of their time in behalf of the world they would hardly get through before night would Come when no man Could work."[5]

President Joseph Fielding Smith wrote of these four destroying angels: "These are now at work in the earth on their sacred mission."[6] And on several occasions before that, President Wilford Woodruff spoke to large audiences about these four angels. On Sunday, June 24, 1894, President Woodruff said to a group of temple workers in the Tabernacle that "those angels have left the portals of heaven, and they stand over this people and this nation now, and are hovering over the earth waiting to pour out the judgments. And from this very day they shall be poured out. Calamities and troubles are increasing in the earth, and there is a meaning to these things. Remember this, and reflect upon these matters. If you do your duty, and I do my duty, we'll have protection, and shall pass through the afflictions in peace and safety.

---

5. Ehat and Cook, *Words of Joseph Smith*, 318–19.
6. *Church History and Modern Revelation*, 1:300–301. Other apostolic witnesses have declared that these angels have begun their mission. Said Elder Bruce R. McConkie: "Peace has been taken from the earth, the angels of destruction have begun their work, and their swords shall not be sheathed until the Prince of Peace comes to destroy the wicked and usher in the great Millennium." "Stand Independent above All Other Creatures," *Ensign*, May 1979, 93.

Read the scriptures and the revelations. . . . It's by the power of the gospel that we shall escape."[7]

Less than a month later, President Woodruff once again spoke of these four angels. On July 15, 1894, again in the Tabernacle, President Woodruff taught: "These angels that have been held for many years in the temple of our God have got their liberty to go out and commence their mission and their work in the earth, and they are here today on the earth. I feel bold in saying this to the Latter-day Saints. There is meaning in these judgments. The word of the Lord cannot fall unfulfilled."[8] In yet another discourse, he cited Doctrine and Covenants 86:5–7 and said: "I want to bear testimony to this congregation, and to the heavens and the earth, that the day is come when those angels are privileged to go forth and commence their work. They are laboring in the United States of America; they are laboring among the nations of the earth; and they will continue."[9]

In his June 24, 1894, address, President Woodruff spoke of how the Saints would receive protection from the four destroying angels: "What protection have this vast body of human being[s] [on earth] to enable them to escape those tremendous judgments, which God has proclaimed shall come to pass and be poured out

7. Gates, "Temple Workers' Excursion," *Young Woman's Journal* 5 (1894): 512–13; see also Stuy, *Collected Discourses,* 4:110.
8. "Revelation and Judgment," *Deseret Weekly* 49 (Aug. 25, 1894): 289–90; see also Woodruff, *Millennial Star* 56 (Oct. 8, 1894): 643; Stuy, *Collected Discourses,* 4:127.
9. *Discourses of Wilford Woodruff,* 252. For other statements by President Woodruff regarding the four angels, see Bateman, *Prophets Have Spoken,* 1:90; Woodruff, Journal, May 1834; May 29, 1847.

upon the wicked in the last days, before the coming of the Son of Man? . . .

"I will answer the question for you. Wherever the eternal, everlasting and holy priesthood or its influence dwells, there is protection and salvation and nowhere else. . . .

"The Lord revealed to Joseph Smith the prophet, and said that angels were standing in the Temple in Heaven, holding in their hands sharp sickles, and crying unto God day and night, saying let us go down and reap down the fields. . . . I now bear testimony to this assembly that that day has come. These destroying Angels are sent forth to visit the earth and have commenced to pour out the judgments of God upon the wicked, and will continue until the scene is wound up and all fulfilled that God has promised. Therefore judgment awaits the wicked."[10] In sum, the "eternal, everlasting and holy priesthood" and its influence will provide "protection and salvation" from God's destroying angels to many of the earth's inhabitants in the last days.

---

10. Journal, June 24, 1894.

Chapter 23

ANGELS MAY SAVE
LIVES IN PERIL

*[We] might have standing by us in our hour
of peril or great need an angel of God.*

PRESIDENT HAROLD B. LEE

O ccasionally the angelic purpose is to warn," taught Elder
Jeffrey R. Holland.[1] Indeed, we have a number of scriptural
accounts in which angels warned mortals or saved them from
peril or even death. President Harold B. Lee confirmed that angels may, on occasion, save mortals from perilous circumstances:
"If our problems be too great for human intelligence or too much
for human strength, we too, if we are faithful and appeal rightly
unto the source of divine power, might have standing by us in our
hour of peril or great need an angel of God."[2]

The Lord sent two angels (Hebrew, *malachim;* see Genesis
19:1, 15) to destroy the wicked people of the city of Sodom.[3]
Before destroying the city, however, the angels provided

Stand Ye in Holy Places, 103; or *Teachings of Harold B. Lee,* 614.

1. "The Ministry of Angels," *Ensign,* Nov. 2008, 29.
2. *Teachings of Harold B. Lee,* 614.
3. Joseph Smith refers to these angels in *History of the Church,* 5:31.

protection to Lot, his wife, and his two daughters. When the wicked men of the city attempted to assault Lot and his family, the angels "smote the men that were at the door of the house with blindness, both small and great: so that they wearied themselves to find the door" (Genesis 19:11). The angels then instructed Lot to gather his family and to leave the city because, they said, "We will destroy this place. . . . the Lord hath sent us to destroy it. . . . And when the morning arose, then the angels hastened Lot, saying, Arise, take thy wife, and thy two daughters, which are here; lest thou be consumed in the iniquity of the city" (Genesis 19:13–15).

At the time of the Exodus from Egypt, the militarily inexperienced children of Israel were no match for Pharaoh's well-equipped and disciplined army. With its state-of-the-art chariots, horses, horsemen, and armed forces, Egypt was a world power. To make matters worse, many of the Israelites had the mind-set of slaves. But the Lord's angel wielded greater power than all of Egypt with its armies and chariots. God had promised Moses, "The Lord shall fight for you, and ye shall hold your peace" (Exodus 14:14).

The night before the Israelites fled through the Red Sea, this angel protected the Israelites: "And the angel of God, which went before the camp of Israel, removed and went behind them" (Exodus 14:19). The Lord also empowered this angel to protect Moses and Israel as they journeyed to the promised land. "Behold, I send an Angel before thee, to keep thee in the way, and to bring thee into the place which I have prepared. . . . For mine Angel shall go before thee, and bring thee in unto the Amorites, and the Hittites, and the Perizzites, and the Canaanites, the Hivites, and the Jebusites: and I will cut them off" (Exodus 23:20, 23). Furthermore, the Lord's name would be in this angel, meaning the angel would possess full authority from God. The Lord instructed Moses: "Beware of [this angel], and obey his voice, provoke him not; for he will not pardon your transgressions: for my name is in him. But if thou shalt indeed obey his voice, and do all that I speak; then I will be an enemy unto thine enemies, and an adversary unto thine adversaries" (Exodus 23:21–22).

Another Old Testament passage refers to an angel who helps in time of peril. The author of Psalm 35 pleaded with the Lord in prayer, asking for help when his enemies fought against him: "Plead my cause, O Lord, with them that strive with me: fight against them that fight against me . . . and let the angel of the Lord chase them. Let their way be dark and slippery: and let the angel of the Lord persecute [Hebrew, *pursue*] them" (Psalm 35:1–6). In this psalm, the one praying also seeks for the help of angels: To *chase* and *pursue* suggests that the enemies (in this case, the enemies of the psalmist) are fleeing from the angel.

The Lord's angel instructed and protected the prophet Elijah from Ahaziah, the king of Israel, who sought him. First, the king sent messengers to meet with Elijah, and "the angel of the Lord said to Elijah the Tishbite, Arise, go up to meet the messengers of the king of Samaria" (2 Kings 1:3). Then the king sent fifty trained soldiers with their captain to capture Elijah, who was sitting on a hilltop. These soldiers were unsuccessful, so the king sent a second captain with fifty soldiers. They also failed. So the king sent a third captain with fifty soldiers. During the course of these events, the angel of the Lord gave Elijah instructions and in the end directed him to accompany the third captain and his soldiers to meet the king. The angel said to Elijah, "Go down with him [the third captain]: be not afraid of him. And he arose, and went down with him unto the king" (2 Kings 1:15). With his statement, "Be not afraid of him," the angel assured the prophet that he (the angel) would protect Elijah when he met with the king (2 Kings 1:9–15).

Likewise, the New Testament record tells us of angels who saved mortals from danger. For example, when Herod Agrippa I, of the wicked Herodian family, was persecuting Christians, he killed James and imprisoned Peter (Acts 12:1–3), intending to slay Peter right after Easter. Both the killing of Peter and the timing of it would magnify Herod's popularity among the many non-Christians of the nation. Herod had undoubtedly heard of the great power of the apostles and the miracles that they had performed, so he kept Peter under heavy guard. Sixteen ("four quaternions") skilled and disciplined soldiers guarded the chief apostle. Two soldiers slept on either side of the apostle at night to keep close watch. Peter was secured with two chains that not only bound his movements but also rattled or clattered whenever he shifted his body. Trained doorkeepers watched the prison doors, and Peter was secured within two wards—prison cells or sections. In case all of these precautions were not enough, an iron gate blocked the outer area of the prison. In spite of these measures to keep Peter locked up, the Lord's angel would set him free.

While Peter was in prison, the Saints were praying for their leader: "Prayer was made without ceasing of the church unto God for him" (Acts 12:5). To add to the intensity of the situation, Herod intended to take Peter from prison to slay him the very next day, but the prayers and faith of the Saints resulted in the appearance of an angel just in time. Acts 12 states: "When Herod would have brought him forth, the same night Peter was sleeping between two soldiers, bound with two chains: and the keepers before the door kept the prison. And, behold, the angel of the Lord came upon him, and a light shined in the prison: and he smote Peter on the side, and raised him up, saying, Arise up quickly. And his chains fell off from his hands. And the angel said unto him, Gird thyself, and bind on thy sandals. And so he did. And he saith unto him, Cast thy garment about thee, and follow me. And he went out, and followed him; and wist not that it was true which was done by the angel; but thought he saw a vision. When they were past the first and the second ward, they came unto the iron gate that leadeth unto the city; which opened to them of his own accord: and they went out, and passed on through one street; and forthwith the angel departed from him" (Acts 12:6–10).

This narrative shows that the angel performed at least five miracles: (1) He appeared in the prison, inside locked doors and an iron gate, despite the watchful eyes of doorkeepers and sixteen soldiers; (2) the angel's glory resulted in a light shining within the prison; (3) the angel caused Peter's chains to fall from his hands without awakening the soldiers; (4) the angel escorted Peter "past the first and the second ward" without alerting the doorkeepers and guards; and (5) when the angel and Peter arrived at the iron gate, it opened without human assistance. In sum, the Lord's angel helped Peter escape from prison despite all the precautions taken by King Herod Agrippa.

In the Book of Mormon, we read that an angel saved Nephi, the son of Lehi, from brutalization and possible death at the hands of his two older brothers. The story takes place early in the Book of Mormon after Lehi sent his sons back to Jerusalem to obtain the brass plates from Laban. Laban responded to their request by attempting to kill Lehi's sons, but they fled from Laban and hid in a cave, or a cavity of a rock. This series of events angered Laman and Lemuel, who consequently spoke "many hard words" against Nephi and Sam. Nephi recorded: "They did smite us even with a rod. And it came to pass as they smote us with a rod, behold, an angel of the Lord came and stood before them, and he spake unto them, saying: Why do ye smite your younger brother with a rod? Know ye not that the Lord hath chosen him to be a ruler over you, and this because of your iniquities? Behold ye shall go up to Jerusalem again, and the Lord will deliver Laban into your hands. And after the angel had spoken unto us, he departed" (1 Nephi 3:28–31).

The preceding stories—Lot and his family in Sodom, Elijah and the king of Samaria, Peter in prison, Nephi and Sam being smitten with a rod—all pertain to temporal perils and dangers. The next story, however, pertains not just to temporal danger but also to spiritual peril—three angels save two of God's special servants from a host of wicked spirits.

President Wilford Woodruff and Elder George A. Smith, then members of the Quorum of the Twelve Apostles serving as missionaries in London, England, in October 1840, had an extraordinary experience involving angels. More than fifty years later, Wilford Woodruff, by then president of the Church, recounted the story: "We sat up one night till about 11 o'clock, talking about the Gospel of Christ, and then went to bed. The room in which we slept was small; there was about three and a half feet between our cots. Those spirits were gathered together in that room and sought to destroy us. They fell upon us with the determination to take our lives. The distress, the suffering and the horror that rested upon me I never experienced before nor since. While in this condition a spirit said to me, 'Pray to the Lord.' . . . I prayed the Lord, in the name of Jesus Christ, to preserve our lives. While I was praying, the door opened and three messengers entered, and the room was filled with light equal to the blazing of the sun at mid-day. Those messengers were all dressed in robes of immortal beings. Who they were I do not know. They laid hands upon me and my companion, and rebuked those evil powers, and we were saved. From that hour to this day, not only our lives were saved, but those powers were rebuked by the angels of God so that no Elder since has been tormented with them in London."[4]

President Woodruff's testimony of what happened that night in London reveals significant truths regarding angels: Angels saved the lives of Elders Woodruff and Smith; the angels laid their hands on them, signifying that the angels were likely translated or resurrected personages; the angels' glory was of such brilliance

---

4. *Deseret Weekly* 53 (Oct. 24, 1896): 577; see also Stuy, *Collected Discourses,* 5:199. President Woodruff recorded this account in his journal, Oct. 18, 1840. He retold this story many times; see, for example, *Deseret Weekly* 53 (Nov. 7, 1896): 642; Stuy, *Collected Discourses,* 5:236.

that their light filled the room "equal to the blazing of the sun at mid-day"; the three angels had much greater power than a host of evil spirits; the power of these three angels protected numerous other missionaries, because "no Elder since has been tormented with [evil spirits] in London"; and the angels were dressed in "robes of immortal beings."

On another occasion, while in Arkansas, President Wilford Woodruff was saved by an angel from a violent apostate and a mob. A man named Akeman had apostatized from the Church, cursed Joseph Smith, the Twelve Apostles, and others, and was full of rage. But neither Akeman nor his mob could harm Wilford and his companion.[5]

At least two apostles in our dispensation have publicly shared dreams that featured angels who saved them from peril. President Heber C. Kimball recorded: "I was in a great water, swimming, and had swam away, trying to make land, although I saw no land, until I had become weary and tired, when I began to sink; then an angel came to me and placed his hand under my chin, for some time keeping me from sinking, until I had rested and gained strength; he blessed me and said, 'Brother Heber, you shall now have strength to swim ashore.' I again began to swim, and it appeared as though every time I stretched forth my arms and feet, I would move rods at each stroke, and continued doing so until I reached land."[6]

President George Q. Cannon had a similar experience at the

---

5. Woodruff, *Deseret Weekly* 53 (Nov. 7, 1896): 641–42; see also Stuy, *Collected Discourses*, 5:234–35; Woodruff, *Leaves from My Journal*, 24–26.
6. Whitney, *Life of Heber C. Kimball*, 120.

beginning of his first mission. In November 1850, he and nine other elders were headed to the Sandwich Islands (Hawaii). But their ship, said President Cannon, was "wind-bound in the Bay of San Francisco, and we had been thus delayed for nearly a week near the Golden Gate in consequence of head winds. I dreamed one night that this party of brethren were heaving at the wind-lass, having a rope attached to it reaching forward to the anchor at the bow of the vessel. We were working with all our might endeavoring to raise the anchor, but seemingly we made but little progress. While thus engaged I thought the Prophet Joseph came from the after part of the vessel . . . and tapping me on the shoulder told me to go with him. I went, and he climbed on to the forecastle which was higher than the main deck and on a level with the bulwarks, and there he knelt down, also telling me to kneel down with him. He prayed according to the order of prayer which is revealed. After prayer, he arose upon his feet. 'Now,' said he, 'George, take hold of that rope—the rope we had been pulling on with all our might. I took hold of it, and with the greatest ease and without the least effort, the anchor was raised.' 'Now,' said he, 'let this be a lesson to you; remember that great things can be accomplished through the power of prayer and the exercise of faith in the right way.'"[7]

7. *Journal of Discourses*, 22:289.

Chapter 24

ANGELS WHO PROTECT

❧❦❧

*God's holy angels are ever on call
to help us. . . . When we are faithful,
He and His angels will help us.*

ELDER RUSSELL M. NELSON

The Old Testament account that details Daniel's being thrown to the lions features an angel who protected the prophet's life. The setting pertains to King Darius's leaders, officers, and governors, who convinced the king to sign a decree that forbade anyone to pray to his god or deity. Anyone who disobeyed the decree would be cast into a den of lions (see Daniel 6:7–9). Although Daniel knew about the decree, he chose to hearken to God's commandment to call upon him in prayer not just once but three times daily (see Daniel 6:10). Daniel's actions resulted in his being cast into a den of lions. To ensure that Daniel would not escape from the wild animals, "a stone was brought, and laid upon the mouth of the den; and the king sealed it with his own signet, and with the signet of his lords; that the purpose might

---

"Face the Future with Faith," *Ensign,* May 2011, 35.

not be changed concerning Daniel" (Daniel 6:17). That the lions were fierce and ravenous is clear from Daniel 6:24, which states that the lions would break into pieces all the bones of their victims, even before the victims could reach the den's bottom.

Because of Daniel's faith and righteousness, the Lord's angel protected him from a horrific death. Daniel testified, "My God hath sent his angel, and hath shut the lions' mouths, that they have not hurt me: forasmuch as before him innocency was found in me" (Daniel 6:22). Not only are angels immune to destruction by lions but angels also have the power to protect others from such destruction.

Beyond the narrative of Daniel are numerous other accounts of protecting angels, both in ancient times as well as in our own dispensation. In recent decades, many leaders of our Church—including President David O. McKay, President Joseph Fielding Smith, President Harold B. Lee, Elder Bruce R. McConkie, Elder Dallin H. Oaks, Elder Robert D. Hales, President Gordon B. Hinckley, and President Thomas S. Monson—have referred to angels who protect or guard mortals.[1] Several prophets and apostles of the nineteenth and early twentieth centuries also spoke or wrote of protecting angels, including the Prophet Joseph Smith, President Brigham Young, President Wilford Woodruff, Elder Orson Hyde, Elder Orson Pratt, Elder Parley P. Pratt, President

---

1. For example, Smith, *Doctrines of Salvation*, 1:54; McConkie, *Mormon Doctrine*, 341–42; Thomas S. Monson, "Miracles—Then and Now," *Ensign*, Nov. 1992, 68.

Joseph F. Smith, Elder James E. Talmage, Elder Hyrum G. Smith, Elder Orson F. Whitney, and Elder John A. Widtsoe.[2]

ANGELS PROTECT SOME INDIVIDUALS FROM VARIOUS FORCES OF EVIL

Joseph Smith recorded an experience that occurred at the Kirtland Temple, when one of the worshippers saw six angels surround the temple to protect worshippers from the power of the devil and his hosts: "When the Twelve and the seven presidents were through with their sealing prayer, I called upon President Sidney Rigdon to seal them with uplifted hands; and when he had done this, and cried hosanna, that all the congregation should join him, and shout hosanna to God and the Lamb, and glory to God in the highest. It was done so, and Elder Roger Orton saw a mighty angel riding upon a horse of fire, with a flaming sword in his hand, followed by five others, encircle the house, and protect the Saints, even the Lord's anointed, from the power of Satan and a host of evil spirits, which were striving to disturb the Saints." Not only did Elder Orton envision protecting angels, but President William Smith, a member of the Twelve, "saw the heavens opened, and the Lord's host protecting the Lord's anointed."[3]

In general conference of April 2011, Elder Russell M. Nelson

---

2. *Teachings of the Prophet Joseph Smith,* 368–69; *History of the Church,* 2:288; Young, *Journal of Discourses,* 13:76; Woodruff, Journal, Mar. 18, 1860; Orson Pratt, *Journal of Discourses,* 2:343–44; Pratt, *Key to the Science of Theology,* 120–23; Hyde, as recorded in Woodruff, Journal, May 3, 1846; Talmage, *Millennial Star* 55 (July 10, 1893): 446 (see also Stuy, *Collected Discourses,* 3:291); Smith, *From Prophet to Son,* 39–40; Widtsoe, *Gospel Interpretations,* 28–29; *Evidences and Reconciliations,* 403.
3. *History of the Church,* 2:386–87.

spoke of "physical and spiritual protection" and angels that will help the faithful. He admonished us: "Teach of faith to know that obedience to the commandments of God will provide physical and spiritual protection. And remember, God's holy angels are ever on call to help us. The Lord so declared: 'I will go before your face. I will be on your right hand and on your left, and my Spirit shall be in your hearts, and mine angels round about you, to bear you up.' What a promise! When we are faithful, He and His angels will help us."[4]

Elder Dallin H. Oaks also taught of angels who protect in the context of mortality's hardships and trials. "All over the world, faithful Latter-day Saints are protected from the powers of the evil one and his servants until they have finished their missions in mortality. For some the mortal mission is brief. . . . But for most of us the mortal journey is long, and we continue our course with the protection of guardian angels."[5]

After Elder Robert D. Hales experienced several significant trials of health, he reported in general conference: "[I] learned that I would not be left alone to meet these trials and tribulations but that guardian angels would attend me. There were some that were near angels in the form of doctors, nurses, and most of all my sweet companion, Mary. And on occasion, when the Lord so desired, I was to be comforted with visitations of heavenly hosts that brought comfort and eternal reassurances in my time of need."[6]

4. "Face the Future with Faith," *Ensign*, May 2011, 35.
5. "Bible Stories and Personal Protection," *Ensign*, Nov. 1992, 39.
6. "The Covenant of Baptism: To Be in the Kingdom and of the Kingdom," *Ensign*, Nov. 2000, 6.

WHO MAY SERVE AS A PROTECTING ANGEL?

Those who have passed beyond the veil may at times protect mortals, a sweet and reassuring doctrine taught by President Harold B. Lee, Elder Hyrum G. Smith, and others. "*Those in the spirit world may be guardian angels to those in mortality,*" explained President Lee. "Who are guardian angels? Well, it would appear that someone who is quickened by some influence, not yet celestialized, is permitted to come back as a messenger for the purpose of working with and trying to aid those who are left behind."[7] Sometimes protecting angels are kindred or relatives of those whom they protect. During the October 1928 general conference, Elder Hyrum G. Smith, the patriarch to the Church, explained that "the spirits of our departed loved ones, as well as other spirits, may be appointed to act as our guardian angels."[8]

To illustrate that protecting angels at times are none other than departed loved ones, President Harold B. Lee shared the following story: "I heard this little flaxen-haired girl sing 'I Am a Child of God.' 'Lead me, guide me, walk beside me, help me find the way.' The first time I heard it, this little girl sang it to her mother's accompaniment. Now [her] mother is gone. But the mother came to this little girl in such a vivid dream that she said the next morning, 'Oh, Mother was with us. We saw her in the family room, and I said, "Oh, Mother, you're not dead." And she said, "No, my dear, I am not dead. I am very much alive. You won't be able to see me all the time, but I won't be far away from

---

7. *Teachings of Harold B. Lee,* 59.
8. Conference Report, Oct. 1928, 82.

you, my dear.'" And with that childish assurance, the little girl is now growing to womanhood. Lead me, guide me, walk beside me, help me find the way. Guardian angels? Don't you mistake it. It isn't your father and mother who will be far away from you, children; it will be you who keep them far away."[9]

Once, when speaking at a funeral, President Lee stated: "Let this [funeral] not be a time of abject sorrow, but realize that your father might return to you as your holy guardian, limited in his scope but there when you need him the most. How do you know but that he may be very close and very near on occasions when such a messenger would be very valuable?"[10]

On April 24, 1918, Elder Orson F. Whitney recorded an experience in which his deceased wife appeared to him as a protecting angel. Early one morning, while Elder Whitney was "half asleep, half awake" in his bed, he became aware that someone was in his room. At first he thought that whoever was in the room may have intended to harm him, so he thought to "lie perfectly still in order to be safe." But moments later he realized that the person in his room was none other than his deceased wife: "Presently I saw my wife Zina, who had been dead for eighteen years. . . . It was all so real. I could not doubt that she was actually there, a guardian angel, watching over her children and me."[11]

In the October 1968 general conference, President David O. McKay spoke of angels who protect. He recalled a "remarkable" meeting he attended in Glasgow, Scotland, in 1899, in which

9. *Teachings of Harold B. Lee*, 59.
10. *Teachings of Harold B. Lee*, 60.
11. *Through Memory's Halls*, 413; see also Kimball, *Journal of Discourses*, 6:127.

"everybody felt the rich outpouring of the Spirit of the Lord. . . . During the progress of the meeting, an elder on his own initiative arose and said, 'Brethren, there are angels in this room.'

"Strange as it may seem, the announcement was not startling; indeed, it seemed wholly proper, though it had not occurred to me there were divine beings present. I only knew that I was over-flowing with gratitude for the presence of the Holy Spirit.

"I was profoundly impressed, however, when President James L. McMurrin, president of the European Mission, arose and confirmed that statement by pointing to one brother sitting just in front of me and saying, 'Yes, brethren, there are angels in this room, and one of them is the guardian angel to that young man sitting there,' and he designated one who afterward became a patriarch in the Woodruff Stake of the Church, John Young.

"Pointing to another elder, he said, 'And one is the guardian angel of that young man there,' and he singled out one whom I had known from childhood, David Eccles. Tears were rolling down the cheeks of both of these missionaries—not in sorrow or grief, but as an expression of the overflowing Spirit. Indeed, we were all weeping."[12]

---

12. Conference Report, Oct. 1968, 86.

Chapter 25

THE ARMIES OF ANGELS AND THE LORD OF HOSTS

❧❧❧

Michael, the seventh angel, even the archangel, shall
gather together his armies, even the hosts of heaven.

DOCTRINE & COVENANTS 88:112

The scriptural expression "Lord of hosts" (Hebrew, *Yahweh Sabaoth*) occurs 265 times in the Hebrew Bible (the Old Testament), and the expression "Lord God of hosts" occurs 18 times.[1] The Hebrew words underlying the English term "Lord of hosts" may also be translated as "Lord of armies"; this phrase is used to refer not only to the armies of ancient Israel (1 Samuel 17:45) but also to the heavenly armies of angels. A prominent Hebrew-English lexicon explains that "Lord of armies" sometimes refers to "the heavenly beings making up the heavenly household of Yahweh," or "the heavenly entourage of Yahweh."[2] Further,

---

1. See Koehler and Baumgartner, *Hebrew and Aramaic Lexicon*, 2:996.
2. Koehler and Baumgartner, *Hebrew and Aramaic Lexicon*, 2:995, citing
   1 Kings 22:19; 2 Chronicles 18:18; Psalm 103:21; 148:2; see also Brown,
   Driver, and Briggs, *Hebrew and English Lexicon*, 839, "host (organized body)
   of angels," citing 1 Kings 22:19; 2 Chronicles 18:18; Nehemiah 9:6; Psalms
   103:21; 148:2; and Joshua 5:14–15, which refers to a "theophanic angel."

under the heading "Sabaoth," the LDS Bible Dictionary reads: "*Hosts.* The Lord of Sabaoth was a title of Jehovah; the hosts were the armies of Israel (1 Sam. 17:45), but also included the angelic armies of heaven." In sum, the Lord of hosts is the Lord of the heavenly armies of angels; under the leadership of the Lord and Michael the archangel, the heavenly armies of angels battle against various forces of evil.

Who is the *captain* of the armies of Israel? It is none other than Jehovah himself, who appeared to Joshua and identified himself as "captain of the host of the Lord" (Joshua 5:13–15). During the Old Testament period, as long as the children of Israel remained faithful to the Lord, he would fight in their battles and wars (Joshua 10:42). He was their "man of war" (Exodus 15:3; cf. Isaiah 42:13). "Who is this King of glory? The Lord strong and mighty, the Lord mighty in battle" (Psalm 24:8). Joshua 23:10 states, "One man of you shall chase a thousand: for the Lord your God, he it is that fighteth for you." And David warned Goliath that "the battle is the Lord's and he will give you into our hands" (1 Samuel 17:47). The testimony of the scriptural record—especially the books of Numbers, Deuteronomy, Joshua, Judges, and Samuel—shows that God intervened during wartime on behalf of the children of Israel when they remained faithful (for example, see Exodus 14:27; Joshua 10:5–14, 30, 32; 11:8; 1 Samuel 7:3–13; 2 Kings 6:8–23; 2 Kings 6:24–7:16; 19:14–36; and 2 Chronicles 20:1–26).

The Lord of hosts of the Old Testament is still active in the world today; he still leads his heavenly host. President Brigham Young explained, "When the Lord commands those invisible beings, shall I say, those who have had their resurrection?—yes, millions and millions more than the inhabitants of this earth, they can fight your battles."[3]

President Heber C. Kimball understood that there are armies of angels who protect God's people: "If evil spirits could come to me, cannot ministering spirits and angels also come from God? Of course they can, and . . . they can rush as an army going to battle. . . . That is the God whom I serve, one who has millions of angels at His command. . . . We do not see them, but they are here watching us. . . . The Lord has hosts of angels who are qualified to defend us, and they have information enough to march armies and to select leaders to lead them against the enemy of the Saints."[4]

This statement is in harmony with an awe-inspiring experience of Heber C. and Vilate Kimball. On the night of September 22, 1827, Heber, Vilate, and others saw an army in the sky. A neighbor had awakened Heber, who in turn awakened Vilate. They went outside and looked at the starry night. "It was one of the most beautiful starlight nights, so clear we could see to pick up a pin." He stated that they saw a bow form in the sky, and "it grew wide enough to contain twelve men abreast. In this bow an army moved, commencing from the east and marching to the west. They continued marching until they reached the western horizon. They moved in platoons, and walked so close that the rear ranks trod in the steps of their file leaders, until the whole bow was literally crowded with soldiers. . . .

3. *Discourses of Brigham Young*, 42.
4. *Journal of Discourses*, 3:229–30.

"We . . . could discern the form and features of the men. The most profound order existed throughout the entire army. When the foremost man stepped, every man stepped at the same time. I could hear their steps. When the front rank reached the western horizon, a battle ensued, as we could hear the report of the arms, and the rush.

"No man could judge of my feelings when I beheld that army of men, as plainly as ever I saw armies of men in the flesh; it seemed as though every hair of my head was alive. This scenery we gazed upon for hours, until it began to disappear.

"After I became acquainted with Mormonism, I learned that this took place the same evening that Joseph Smith received the records of the Book of Mormon from the angel Moroni, who had held those records in his possession." There were other witnesses to this event, and "the next night similar scenery was beheld in the west, by the neighbors, representing armies of men who were engaged in battle."[5]

Joseph Smith recorded the accounts of three people who saw heavenly armies—Roger Orton, William Smith, and Joseph's scribe, who "saw, in a vision, the armies of heaven protecting the Saints in their return to Zion."[6]

John the Revelator also saw heavenly armies in vision. He described Jesus Christ's second coming as a spectacular scene: "I saw heaven opened, and behold a white horse; and he that sat upon him was called Faithful and True, and in righteousness he

---

5. Whitney, *Life of Heber C. Kimball,* 15–17; see also McConkie, *Angels,* 100; Tullidge, *Women of Mormondom,* 107–9.
6. *History of the Church,* 2:386–87; 2:381.

doth judge and make war. . . . And he was clothed with a vesture dipped in blood: . . . And the armies which were in heaven followed him upon white horses, clothed in fine linen, white and clean" (Revelation 19:11–14). At his second coming, Jesus will lead his armies and make war against the world and against evil. He and his armies will be victorious.

Chapter 26

ANGELS AS SENTINELS PROTECTING SACRED SPACE

Angels . . . stand as sentinels.

PRESIDENT BRIGHAM YOUNG

Some angels serve as sentinels who guard the way back to heaven, thus preventing unworthy or unauthorized persons from entering heaven. Through the years he was president of the Church, Brigham Young taught Church members about these sentinels. On April 6, 1853, the day that the First Presidency and the Church patriarch, John Smith (brother of Joseph Smith Sr.), laid the southeast cornerstone of the Salt Lake Temple, President Young taught that the "ordinances in the House of the Lord . . . are necessary for you, after you have departed this life, to enable you to walk back to the presence of the Father, passing the angels who stand as sentinels."[1]

President Young taught his audience about these sentinels on

Journal of Discourses, 2:31.

1. *Journal of Discourses,* 2:31. Many Church authorities have cited President Young's statement. See, for example, Spencer W. Kimball, "The Things of Eternity—Stand We in Jeopardy?" *Ensign,* Jan. 1977, 6; David B. Haight, "Come to the House of the Lord," *Ensign,* May 1992, 15–16; Boyd K.

other occasions. On December 3, 1854, he spoke of the "laws and ordinances, by which we can be prepared to pass from one gate to another, and from one sentinel to another, until we go into the presence of our Father and God."[2] On May 24, 1863, President Young spoke of those who would become worthy "to pass by the porters through the door into the celestial kingdom."[3] And again, on February 16, 1868, he taught, "It is absolutely necessary that the Saints should receive the further ordinances of the house of God before this short existence shall come to a close, that they may be prepared and fully able to pass all the sentinels leading into the celestial kingdom and into the presence of God."[4]

Joseph Smith's revelation on marriage refers to angels who are appointed to serve as sentinels. Although sentinels are not explicitly mentioned, the revelation brings them to mind. When a marriage "is not sealed by the Holy Spirit of promise, through him whom I have . . . appointed unto this power, then it is not valid neither of force when they are out of the world, because they are not joined by me, saith the Lord, neither by my word; when they are out of the world it cannot be received there, because the angels and the gods are appointed there, by whom they cannot pass;

Packer, "Come to the Temple," *Ensign,* Oct. 2007, 20–21; and Russell M. Nelson, "Prepare for the Blessings of the Temple," *Ensign,* Oct. 2010, 42.

2. *Journal of Discourses,* 2:139. Less than a year later, President Young spoke of these sentinels again. *Journal of Discourses,* 2:315.
3. *Journal of Discourses,* 10:172.
4. *Journal of Discourses,* 12:163–64.

they cannot, therefore, inherit my glory; for my house is a house of order, saith the Lord God" (D&C 132:18).

CHERUBIM AS GUARDIANS

Symbolic representations of cherubim in the tabernacle of Moses and in the temple of Solomon portrayed them as divine protectors or guardians. For example, representations of the cherubim were embroidered into the walls and veil of the tabernacle (Exodus 26:1, 31; 36:8, 35) and carved into the walls, doors, and panels of the temple of Solomon (1 Kings 6:29–35; 7:29–36).[5] In addition, two large cherubim were attached to the ark of the covenant in the holy of holies (Exodus 25:18–22; 37:7–9; 1 Samuel 4:4; 2 Samuel 6:2; 1 Kings 6:23–28; 8:6–7). Ezekiel also refers to cherubim in his description of Jerusalem's future temple (Ezekiel 41:18–25).

Church general authorities have established that cherubim referred to in the scriptures are angels. President Joseph Fielding Smith wrote of the cherubim, "There is no doubt that these were heavenly beings, or angels."[6] These cherubim functioned as divine sentinels, guarding the path that led to the presence of God and preventing unauthorized persons from trespassing. In the Garden of Eden narrative (Genesis 2–3), the primary mission of

---

5. For a discussion of cherubim as guardians, see Parry, "Cherubim," in Welch and Parry, *Tree of Life*, 1–24. The etymology of *cherubim* (from the root *krb)* is uncertain, and most translations of the Bible transliterate rather than translate the word *cherubim*.

6. *Answers to Gospel Questions*, 2:96–97; see also Widtsoe, *Gospel Interpretations*, 27; and Cannon, "The Angels Who Visit Us," *Juvenile Instructor* 26 (1891): 53–54.

the cherubs, together with the flaming sword, was to guard the path that leads to the tree of life. Genesis 3:24 tells us that the Lord God "drove out the man; and he stationed at the east of the garden of Eden cherubim, and a flaming, revolving sword, to guard the path of the tree of life."[7] In other words, God appointed the cherubim and the flaming sword to serve as guards.

Biblical scholar Victor Hamilton wrote that "God stations the cherubim and the fiery, whirling sword east of the garden of Eden to prevent reentry to the garden, as if reentry into the garden is only through an opening on its east side, much as the entrance into the tabernacle-temple complex was by a gate on the eastern side. In such a capacity the cherubim function much like the later Levites who are posted as guards around the tabernacle, and who are to strike down any person who encroaches upon the forbidden sancta (Num. 1:52, 53)."[8] Another scholar, G. von Rad, describes the cherubim as protectors and asserts that the cherubim "had the duty, above all, of protecting sacred regions (1 Kings 6:23 ff.; 8:6 f.)."[9]

Ezekiel, addressing the king of Tyre, twice referred to a "guardian cherub" in the Garden of Eden: "You used to live in Eden, God's garden. . . . With a winged guardian cherub I set you. On God's sacred mountain you lived, and amidst blazing

---

7. Translation mine. The Hebrew verb *shmr,* translated in the King James Version as "to keep," has the sense of "to take care of, preserve, to protect," or "to perform guard duty." Koehler and Baumgartner, *Hebrew and Aramaic Lexicon,* 2:1583. *Shmr* is also used in connection with guarding captives (see Joshua 10:18; 1 Kings 20:39).
8. *Book of Genesis,* 210; see also Waltke and Fredricks, *Genesis,* 96.
9. *Genesis,* 97.

gems you walked about. Your conduct was blameless from the day you were created until wrongdoing was discovered in you. Your extensive trading filled your habitat with violence and you committed sin. So I removed you in your sullied state from the divine mountain, and the guardian cherub banished you from the habitat of the blazing gems" (Ezekiel 28:13–16).[10]

In addition to the reference in Ezekiel to a guardian cherub, biblical scholar James M. Boice maintains that "the 'living creatures' of Revelation 4 and 5 and Isaiah 6 are similar if not identical beings" to the cherubim.[11]

Four beasts—"like angels in their sphere"

In his Revelation, John recorded that he saw the throne of God in heaven, and "round about the throne, were four beasts . . . and they rest not day and night, saying, Holy, holy, holy, Lord God Almighty . . . those beasts give glory and honor and thanks to him that sat on the throne" (Revelation 4:6, 8–9; see also 5:6–14; 6:1–7). John informs us that the four beasts are capable of worshipping God (Revelation 4:8; 5:8–10): They invite John to "come and see" the events pertaining to the first four seals (Revelation 6:1–7), and one of the beasts delivers the "seven golden vials full of the wrath of God" to the seven angels (Revelation 15:7). The four beasts may be akin to those mentioned in Isaiah 6:2–3 and Ezekiel 1:5–14.

---

10. Translation by Allen, *Ezekiel 20–48*, 90–92.

11. *Genesis 1–11*, 1:243. "It is probable that the seraphim of Is 6:2–6 are another form of the cherubim. The Apocalypse of the seals Rev 4–6 combines them in four [creatures]." Brown, Driver, and Briggs, *Hebrew and English Lexicon of the Old Testament*, 501.

The Prophet Joseph Smith taught that these four beasts, or living creatures, "were like angels in their sphere"[12] and that they "lived on another planet than ours."[13] The Prophet also explained that "John heard the words of the beasts giving glory to God, and understood them. God who made the beasts could understand every language spoken by them. The four beasts were four of the most noble animals that had filled the measure of their creation, and had been saved from other worlds, because they were perfect. . . . We are not told where they came from, and I do not know; but they were seen and heard by John praising and glorifying God."[14]

Some biblical commentators place one of the four beasts at each of the four sides of the throne, where they serve as guardians of the throne. This role is similar to that played by the cherubim.[15]

Guardian of the cave in the Hill Cumorah

On December 11, 1869, then-Elder Wilford Woodruff recorded significant portions of President Brigham Young's remarks at a meeting, including President Young's explanation that Joseph Smith did not return the gold plates to the box "from where he had received them. But he went into a cave in the Hill Cumorah with Oliver Cowdery and deposited those plates upon a table or shelf. In that room were deposited a large amount of gold plates, containing sacred records; and when they first visited that room,

12. *History of the Church*, 5:343.
13. *Words of Joseph Smith*, 171.
14. Ehat and Cook, *History of the Church*, 5:343–44.
15. Davis, *Heavenly Court Judgment*, 126–31.

the sword of Laban was hanging upon the wall and when they last visited it, the sword was drawn from the scabbard and lain upon the table, and a messenger who was the keeper of the room informed them that that sword would never be returned to its scabbard until the Kingdom of God was established upon the earth and until it reigned triumphant over every enemy. Joseph Smith said that cave contained tons of choice treasures and records."[16]

---

16. Journal, Dec. 11, 1869. William H. Dame wrote of the angel who was present in the Hill Cumorah cave; see Diary, Jan. 14, 1855, L. Tom Perry Special Collections, Harold B. Lee Library, Brigham Young University, Provo, Utah, cited in Baugh, "Parting the Veil," in Welch and Carlson, *Opening the Heavens*, 301n39.

Chapter 27

KEYS TO DETECTING
FALSE SPIRITS

❧❦

We may look for angels and receive their
ministrations, but we are to try the spirits and
prove them, for it is often the case that men
make a mistake in regard to these things.

JOSEPH SMITH

To increase the number of his own followers and also to attempt to thwart God's divine plan of happiness, Satan and his angels throughout the ages have imitated the things of God. There are many examples of Satan's counterfeits in the world—the fortune teller's crystal ball seems to imitate the Urim and Thummim; false prophets mimic the Lord's prophets; false temples are copies of God's temples; clairvoyants impersonate God's seers; scripture-like texts imitate the revealed word of God; lust and illicit sex are forgeries for true and eternal love; and, observed the Prophet Joseph Smith, magicians, wizards, witches, oracles, necromancers, soothsayers, astrologers, maniacs, and

---

Teachings of the Prophet Joseph Smith, 161.

188

many others aid in the works of Satan.[1] The devil makes counterfeits of anything that is "virtuous, lovely, or of good report or praiseworthy" (Article of Faith 13), including such gospel ordinances as baptism and the Lord's sacrament, true worship, inspired music, prayer, the sanctity of marriage, communications from the Holy Ghost, and much more.

The devil is so devious and cunning that he can even appear as an angel of light. Paul warned the Corinthians, "And no marvel; for Satan himself is transformed into an angel of light" (2 Corinthians 11:14; see also D&C 128:20; Moses 1:11–25). The Prophet Joseph taught plainly, "The devil may appear as an angel of light."[2] And "there have also been ministering angels in the Church which were of Satan appearing as an angel of light."[3] Note carefully the Prophet's language—the devil is not an angel of light, but he may appear as (*like, similar to*) an angel of light. Jacob's language further clarifies that the devil "transformeth himself *nigh* unto an angel of light" (2 Nephi 9:9; italics added). In the Book of Mormon, the anti-Christ Korihor confessed, "The devil hath deceived me; for he appeared unto me in the form of an angel" (Alma 30:53).

On April 1, 1842, Joseph Smith recorded a discourse on the subject of trying the spirits, in which he taught many truths regarding the operations of false spirits. Many of God's children, throughout the ages, have been manipulated by Satan and his falsehoods, counterfeits, false spirits (Satan and his angels),

---

1. *Teachings of the Prophet Joseph Smith,* 208.
2. *History of the Church,* 3:392.
3. *Teachings of the Prophet Joseph Smith,* 214.

and much more. "Nothing is a greater injury to the children of men than to be under the influence of a false spirit when they think they have the Spirit of God," explained Joseph Smith. "Thousands have felt the influence of its terrible power and baneful effects. Long pilgrimages have been undertaken, penances endured, and pain, misery and ruin have followed in their train; nations have been convulsed, kingdoms overthrown, provinces laid waste, and blood, carnage and desolation are habiliments in which it has been clothed."[4]

Evil spirits have been among mortals since the beginning, and they will continue to plague humankind until the Second Coming. "Spirits of all kinds have been manifested, in every age, and almost among all people," explained Joseph Smith. Also, "lying spirits are going forth in the earth. There will be great manifestations of spirits, both false and true." And on April 28, 1842, the Prophet explained to the sisters of the Relief Society, "The devil has great power to deceive" and can "so transform things as to make one gape at those who are doing the will of God."[5]

Because of the devil's many counterfeits and evil manipulations, the Lord has revealed keys by which the devil may be detected. The Church in New Testament times possessed certain keys. For example, the Saints at Ephesus "tried them which say they are apostles, and are not, and hast found them liars" (Revelation 2:2). The Prophet Joseph taught that the apostles in the early Church dealt with "false spirits," and it was "intelligence

---

4. *Teachings of the Prophet Joseph Smith*, 204–5.
5. *Teachings of the Prophet Joseph Smith*, 203, 161, 227.

which God alone could impart to detect false spirits, and to prove what spirits were of God."[6] Paul wrote that the "discerning of spirits" is a gift of the Spirit (1 Corinthians 12:10).

In our dispensation, Joseph Smith taught much on the subject of discerning spirits. In the discourse of April 1, 1842 (mentioned above), the Prophet asserted, "'Try the spirits,' says John, but who is to do it? The learned, the eloquent, the philosopher, the sage, the divine—all are ignorant. . . . One great evil is, that men are ignorant of the nature of spirits: their power, laws, government, intelligence, etc. and imagine that when there is anything like power, revelation, or vision manifested, that it must be of God." Later in the same discourse Joseph Smith asked: "If Satan should appear as one in glory, who can tell his color, his signs, his appearance, his glory, or what is the manner of his manifestation? . . . who can drag into daylight and develop the hidden mysteries of the false spirits that so frequently are made manifest . . . ? We answer that no man can do this without the Priesthood, and having a knowledge of the laws by which spirits are governed; for as no man knows the things of God, but by the Spirit of God, so no man knows the spirit of the devil, and his power and influence, but by possessing intelligence which is more than human. . . .

"A man must have the discerning of spirits before he can drag into daylight this hellish influence and unfold it unto the world in all its soul-destroying, diabolical, and horrid colors."[7]

---

6. *Teachings of the Prophet Joseph Smith*, 202.
7. *Teachings of the Prophet Joseph Smith*, 203–5.

On Sunday, May 1, 1842, Joseph recorded: "I preached in the grove, on the keys of the kingdom, charity, &c. The keys are certain signs and words by which false spirits and personages may be detected from true, which cannot be revealed to the Elders till the Temple is completed. The rich can only get them in the Temple, the poor may get them on the mountain top as did Moses."[8]

How does one discern between a messenger from God and a messenger from the devil? Or how does a mortal try the spirits? Joseph Smith revealed several keys.

OFFERING ONE'S HAND TO THE MESSENGER

If an angel appears to a person and that person cannot determine whether the messenger is from God or Satan, then the person should offer his or her hand to the messenger. The instructions regarding offering one's hand to an angel or spirit were canonized in what is now Doctrine and Covenants 129:

"When a messenger comes saying he has a message from God, offer him your hand and request him to shake hands with you. If he be an angel he will do so, and you will feel his hand. If he be the spirit of a just man made perfect he will come in his glory; for that is the only way he can appear—Ask him to shake hands with you, but he will not move, because it is contrary to the order of heaven for a just man to deceive; but he will still deliver his message. If it be the devil as an angel of light, when you ask him to shake hands he will offer you his hand, and you will not feel anything; you may therefore detect him. These are three

---

8. *History of the Church*, 4:608.

grand keys whereby you may know whether any administration is from God" (D&C 129:4–9).

In summary, then, these are "three grand keys": (1) An angel from God, if he has a body of flesh and bones, will shake hands with the mortal, and the mortal will feel his hand. (2) An angel from God, if he is the "spirit of a just man made perfect," will not shake hands but will deliver his message. (3) If the spirit is a devil, appearing as an angel of light, when the mortal offers his hand, the evil person will respond by offering his hand, but the mortal will not feel it. "The Devil . . . will either shrink back . . . or offer his hand," explained Joseph.[9]

According to William, Joseph Smith taught: "If an Angel or spirit appears offer him your hand; if he is a spirit from God he will stand still and not offer you his hand. If from the Devil he will either shrink back from you or offer his hand, which if he does you will feel nothing, but be deceived. A good Spirit will not deceive."[10]

On June 27, 1839, then-Elder Wilford Woodruff recorded that Joseph Smith instructed the Twelve regarding keys to detecting the devil: "Among the vast number of the Keys of the Kingdom of God Joseph presented the following one to the Twelve for there benefit in there experience & travels in the flesh which is as follows. In order to detect the devel when he transforms himself nigh unto an angel of light. When an angel of God appears unto man face to face in personage & reaches out his hand unto the man & he takes hold of the angels hand & feels a substance the Same as one man would

---

9. Ehat and Cook, *Words of Joseph Smith*, 20n21.
10. Ehat and Cook, *Words of Joseph Smith*, 44.

in shaking hands with another he may then know that it is an angel of God, & he should place all Confidence in him. Such personages or angels are Saints with there resurrected Bodies, but if a personage appears unto man & offers him his hand & the man takes hold of it & he feels nothing or does not sens[e] any substance he may know it is the devel, for when a Saint whose body is not resurrected appears unto man in the flesh he will not offer him his hand for this is against the law given him & in keeping in mind these things we may detec[t] the devel that he decieved us not."[11]

There is a recorded instance of mortals who had a need to test a personage. Joseph Smith referred to Jesus's visitation to his eleven apostles in Jerusalem the day that he was resurrected; the apostles "were terrified and affrighted, and supposed that they had seen a spirit. And he said unto them. . . . Behold my hands and my feet, that it is I myself: handle me, and see; for a spirit hath not flesh and bones, as ye see me have" (Luke 24:37–39). On this occasion, Jesus was offering one of the keys—"to prove spirits." Joseph Smith taught, "But to prove spirits view the Saviour after his resurrection when he appeared unto his disciples. they were afraid and thought they had seen a spirit but he convinces them of their mistake by telling them to handle him for says he a spirit has not flesh and bones as ye see me have."[12]

IF AN ANGEL HAS SANDY-COLORED HAIR

Joseph Smith provided another key when he related a story of a Church member in New York who had envisioned a devil

11. Ehat and Cook, *Words of Joseph Smith*, 6.
12. Ehat and Cook, *Words of Joseph Smith*, 255.

appearing as an angel of light. This devil was so clever and deceptive that he appeared as "a glorious personage"; he was "arrayed in white"; he descended to the mortal; he instructed this Church member "to fear God"; and he spoke "many true things." On the surface, it appeared that this angel was from God, but Joseph Smith detected that the angel was from Satan because of his "sandy colored hair" and because he contradicted a revelation from God.

Joseph related: "There have also been ministering angels in the Church which were of Satan appearing as an angel of light. A sister in the state of New York had a vision, who said it was told her that if she would go to a certain place in the woods, an angel would appear to her. She went at the appointed time, and saw a glorious personage descending, arrayed in white, with sandy colored hair; he commenced and told her to fear God, and said that her husband was called to do great things, but that he must not go more than one hundred miles from home, or he would not return; whereas God had called him to go to the ends of the earth, and he has since been more than one thousand miles from home, and is yet alive. Many true things were spoken by this personage, and many things that were false. How, it may be asked, was this known to be a bad angel? By the color of his hair; that is one of the signs that he can be known by, and by his contradicting a former revelation."[13]

The Lord's angels do not contradict revelations from God; neither do his angels appear with sandy-colored hair.

---

13. *Teachings of the Prophet Joseph Smith*, 214–15.

Unfortunately, we lack sure knowledge regarding what the color *sandy* meant at the time of Joseph Smith.

THE APPEARANCE OF A DOVE

Joseph Smith provided yet another important key regarding the discerning of messengers from the other world. On March 21, 1841, he instructed his listeners that a dove that accompanies an angel is a certain sign that angel is from God: "The dove which sat upon his shoulder [see Matthew 3:16] was a sure testimony that he was of God. Brethren, be not deceived nor doubtful of this fact: a spirit of a good man or an angel from heaven who has not a body will never undertake to shake hands with you, for he knows you cannot perceive his touch, and never will extend his hand, but any spirit or body that is attended by a dove you may know to be a pure spirit. Thus you may in some measure detect the spirits who may come unto you."[14]

Beyond the keys that have been revealed concerning discerning the spirits, one may also respond to the following common-sense questions posed by Joseph Smith. With regard to persons who have been manipulated by false spirits, the Prophet Joseph Smith asked, "Is there any intelligence communicated? Are the curtains of heaven withdrawn, or the purposes of God developed? Have they seen and conversed with an angel—or have the glories of futurity burst upon their view?"[15]

---

14. Ehat and Cook, *Words of Joseph Smith*, 66.
15. *Teachings of the Prophet Joseph Smith*, 204.

Chapter 28

ANGELS EXECUTE JUDGMENTS AND CALAMITIES IN THE LAST DAYS

✥❧◈❧✥

*Yea, well doth he cry, by the voice of his
angels that: I will come down among my people,
with equity and justice in my hands.*

ALMA 10:21

God has commissioned some of his angels to have authority over particular calamities, catastrophes, and disasters in
the last days. These events, which are directed to the wicked, are
collectively called God's judgments and include a variety of such
devastations as earthquakes, tornadoes, famines, wars, pestilences,
scourges, plagues, tsunamis, hail, storms, whirlwinds, hurricanes,
and much more. Many prophets and apostles, both ancient and
modern, have spoken of these judgments.[1]

Why judgments from God? Possible purposes for God's judgments include the following: (1) Judgments are designed to mo-
tivate the wicked to repent; if the wicked do repent and apply the

---

1. See Woodruff, Journal, June 24, 1894. Elder John A. Widtsoe explained, "It
would appear also from numerous statements that angels have often been
sent out to execute judgments upon the wicked." *Gospel Interpretations*, 28.

atonement of Jesus Christ in their lives, then the judgments will have served a great purpose. (2) Judgments bring justice to those who refuse to repent; mercy is part of God's plan of salvation, but so is justice. (3) Judgments also serve to prevent the wicked from continuing in wickedness, which would hurt both them and others. (4) When the righteous witness that God is executing judgments upon the wicked, they are able to determine that God's promises regarding the balance between justice and mercy are being fulfilled; they witness that God is a fair and just God, rewarding the righteous and penalizing the wicked. (5) Judgments cleanse the earth for the sake of the righteous and for the return of Jesus Christ at his second coming.

Despite the horrendous effects of various catastrophes, there is great hope for those who follow Christ and keep his commandments. God, who is perfectly holy, all powerful, and all knowing, uses his perfect wisdom to execute judgments upon the wicked; when he administers justice to the wicked, we can be assured that that is best for both the wicked and the righteous; God is in perfect control of these judgments: He can destroy and save according to his divine plans.

As John sets forth in his Revelation, the temple in heaven is the origin of the judgments (Revelation 14:15, 17; 15:5–6; 16:17). President Wilford Woodruff is likewise a witness that the angels who execute God's judgments would come forth from the temple in heaven. President Woodruff taught: "The Lord revealed to Joseph Smith the prophet, and said that angels were standing in the Temple in Heaven, holding in their hands sharp sickles . . . These destroying Angels are sent forth to visit the earth and have commenced to pour out the judgments of God upon the wicked, and will continue until the scene is wound up and all fulfilled that God has promised. Therefore judgment awaits the wicked."[2]

Knowing that the Lord's judgments originate from his heavenly temple and having a complete understanding that he possesses perfect wisdom and knowledge should bring a certain amount of peace and consolation to the humble followers of truth as they hear of or witness calamities in the last days.

Angels who execute judgments

A number of scriptural passages indicate that certain of the Lord's angels execute judgments upon the wicked. These passages include symbols and figurative language, and we cannot always determine what is symbolic and what is literal; the angels' trumpets and bowls, for example, are probably symbolic rather than literal. We will briefly examine four representative passages: (1) angels as reapers (see Matthew 13); (2) seven angels and God's judgments (see Revelation 8); (3) three angels of judgment (see Revelation 14); and (4) seven angels with seven plagues (see Revelation 15:1–8).

Angels as reapers

After Jesus gave the parable of the wheat and the tares, his disciples asked for an interpretation (see Matthew 13:24–30, 36–43). Jesus's interpretation was plain and to the point: The sower is Christ himself; the field represents the world; the good and bad seed represent the righteous and the wicked people of the world; the enemy represents Satan; the reapers at harvest time are the angels of God; and the harvest symbolizes the end of the world.

---

2. Journal, June 24, 1894.

The Savior stated explicitly: "The reapers are the angels. . . . The Son of man shall send forth his angels, and they shall gather out of his kingdom all things that offend, and them which do iniquity" (Matthew 13:39, 41; see also Joel 3:13; Revelation 14:14–16; D&C 45:2; 56:16). In latter-day revelation the Lord reveals that "the angels are crying unto the Lord day and night, who are ready and waiting to be sent forth to reap down the fields" (D&C 86:5).

SEVEN ANGELS AND GOD'S JUDGMENTS

John the Revelator wrote of seven angels who were preparing to sound their trumpets (see Revelation 8:1–5). After a period of "silence in heaven" (Revelation 8:1), six angels sound their trumpets (see Revelation 8–9) and bring to the earth judgments that warn the wicked to repent and also cleanse the earth for Christ's coming. Finally, the seventh angel sounds his trumpet (see Revelation 11:15–19). Doctrine and Covenants 88:92 states, "And angels shall fly through the midst of heaven, crying with a loud voice, sounding the trump of God, saying: Prepare ye, prepare ye, O inhabitants of the earth; for the judgment of our God is come."

The scriptures tell us the following about the blasts of the seven trumpets: (1) Seven angels who stand before God are each given a trumpet (see Revelation 8:2). They are prepared to sound them (see Revelation 8:6), and then one by one they do so (see Revelation 8:7–8, 10, 12; 9:1, 13–14; 10:7; 11:15). The seven angels will blow their trumpets at some point during the last days to prepare the earth's inhabitants for the Second Coming (see D&C 77:12). (2) The trumpets' blasts bring calamities upon the earth, which warn its inhabitants of greater destructions yet to come when angels pour out of the seven bowls spoken of in Revelation 16. (3) The calamities that accompany the blowing of the trumpets encourage the earth's inhabitants to repent (see Revelation 9:20–21; 16:9, 11, 21). (4) The seven angels spoken of in Revelation may be the same angels as those who blast their trumpets, as prophesied in Doctrine and Covenants 88:94–110.

THREE ANGELS OF JUDGMENT

In his Revelation, John sees three angels who would proclaim or execute judgment upon the world (see Revelation 14:6–13).

The first angel announces judgment. John wrote, "And I saw another angel fly in the midst of heaven, having the everlasting gospel to preach unto them that dwell on the earth, and to every nation, and kindred, and tongue, and people, saying with a loud voice, Fear God, and give glory to him; for *the hour of his judgment is come*" (Revelation 14:6–7; italics added). The Lord also spoke of this angel in Doctrine and Covenants 133:36–40.

The second angel announces the fall of Babylon. John wrote, "And there followed another angel, saying, Babylon is fallen, is fallen, that great city, because she made all nations drink of the wine of the wrath of her fornication" (Revelation 14:8). Whereas anciently Babylon was a literal city, in John's prophecy Babylon is a symbol of the wicked world of today. The wicked, idolatrous, and immoral people of our present world are also denominated Babylon. And her prophetic destiny is to fall and to be destroyed, a destiny that surely will come to pass, as many prophets have foreseen (see Isaiah 21:9; Jeremiah 51:7–8; Daniel 5:25–28).

The third angel announces judgment to those who worship the beast. John wrote, "And the third angel followed them, saying with a loud voice, If any man worship the beast and his image, . . . the same shall drink of the wine of the wrath of God, which is poured out without mixture into the cup of his indignation; and he shall be tormented with fire and brimstone in the presence of the holy angels, and in the presence of the Lamb" (Revelation 14:9–10).

SEVEN ANGELS WITH SEVEN PLAGUES

John saw in his Revelation "seven angels having the seven last plagues," which seven angels will pour out seven final judgments on the earth (Revelation 15:1, 7). These seven last plagues are the Lord's final attempt to cause the hearts of the wicked to be softened and to turn to him. After these plagues will come the fall of Babylon and also the second coming of Christ.

Revelation 15:6 states that "the seven angels came out of the temple, having the seven plagues." The seven angels receive their charge in the heavenly temple and then emerge with the seven plagues. That the judgments come from the temple is a mark of their godly origin. That the seven angels are "clothed in pure and white linen, and having their breasts girded with golden girdles" also indicates that they came out of the heavenly temple. The linen dress of the angels, pure and white, indicates that they hold a sacred and holy office (see Ezekiel 9:2; Daniel 10:5). Linen also suggests the bride of Christ (see Revelation 19:7–8) and the armies of heaven (see Revelation 19:14). The high rank of the angels is implied by the golden girdles (sashes) they wear, which are like that worn by Christ himself (see Revelation 1:13).

Chapter 29

ANGELS AND THE SIGNS OF THE TIMES AND THE SECOND COMING

The Son of man shall come in his glory,
and all the holy angels with him.

MATTHEW 25:31

G od's angels have vital roles in the last days and at the second coming of Jesus Christ.

- An angel heralds the everlasting gospel.
- Angels with trumpets invite people to repent.
- Angels with trumpets gather the elect.
- Angels harvest the wicked.
- Angels announce God's judgments and calamities.
- An angel's trump announces the burning of "the mother of abominations" (D&C 88:94).
- An angel's trump announces, "It is finished" (D&C 88:106).
- Angels announce the Second Coming with the sound of a trump.
- Angels accompany Jesus at his second coming.
- Angels do not know the hour or the day of the Second Coming.

The foregoing roles of angels are related to the signs of the times and the Second Coming. As we read scriptures that speak of angels with trumpets or angels as reapers with sickles, we must remember that there is a great deal of symbolism in these passages. For example, whether the angels sound actual trumpets is unknown. We must, therefore, remain cautious as we strive to understand such passages.

AN ANGEL HERALDS THE EVERLASTING GOSPEL

"And I saw another angel fly in the midst of heaven, having the everlasting gospel to preach unto them that dwell on the earth, and to every nation, and kindred, and tongue, and people, saying with a loud voice, Fear God, and give glory to him; for the hour of his judgment is come: and worship him that made heaven, and earth, and the sea, and the fountains of waters" (Revelation 14:6–7; see also D&C 133:36–40; 77:8; chapter 33 of this volume).

ANGELS WITH TRUMPETS INVITE PEOPLE TO REPENT

Alma, for example, wished that he were an angel who could "go forth and speak with the trump of God, with a voice to shake the earth, and cry repentance unto every people!" (Alma 29:1). See chapters 18 and 33 of this volume.

ANGELS WITH TRUMPETS GATHER THE ELECT

The Lord sends angels to assist in the gathering of his elect before the Second Coming: "The Son of Man shall come, and he shall send his angels before him with the great sound of a trumpet, and they shall gather together the remainder of his elect from the four winds, from one end of heaven to the other" (Joseph Smith–Matthew 1:37).

ANGELS HARVEST THE WICKED

The Prophet Joseph Smith taught that angels have significant roles in the harvest of the last days: "The angels are to have something to do in this great work, for they are the reapers."[1] And also, "the harvest is the end of the world; the reapers are the angels. The end of the world is not come, consequently the harvest. The harvest cannot come without angels; The Son of Man is to send forth his angels. . . . The Son of God will do as he ever has done from the beginning. Send forth his Angels. If the reapers do not come, the wheat cannot be saved."[2]

Revelation 14:17–19 describes the roles of two angels in the harvesting of the wicked: "And another angel came out of the temple which is in heaven, he also having a sharp sickle. And another angel came out from the altar, which had power over fire; and cried with a loud cry to him that had the sharp sickle, saying, Thrust in thy sharp sickle, and gather the clusters of the vine of the earth; for her grapes are fully ripe. And the angel thrust in his sickle into the earth, and gathered the vine of the earth, and cast it into the great winepress of the wrath of God." In this scene, an angel will harvest the wicked as if they were clusters of grapes. Then the angel will cast the wicked into a winepress that represents God's wrath (meaning the execution of his judgments), which, according to justice, exacts the full, terrible payment for sin.

Other scriptural passages use *wheat* and *tares* as symbols to portray the gathering of the righteous (the wheat) and the

---

1. *Teachings of the Prophet Joseph Smith*, 101.
2. Ehat and Cook, *Words of Joseph Smith*, 13.

destruction of the wicked (the burning of the tares). Jesus, for example, used these symbols in one of his parables (see JST, Matthew 13:24–30, 37–43). A latter-day revelation states that "the angels are waiting the great command to reap down the earth, to gather the tares that they may be burned; and, behold, the enemy is combined" (D&C 38:12; see also 86:4–7).

Angels announce God's judgments and calamities

God has commissioned some of his angels to have authority over particular calamities and disasters in the last days. For example, there will be seven angels and God's judgments (see Revelation 8); three angels of judgment (see Revelation 14); and seven angels with seven plagues (see Revelation 15:1–8). See chapter 28 of this volume.

An angel's trump announces the burning of "the mother of abominations"

"And another angel shall sound his trump, saying: That great church, the mother of abominations, that made all nations drink of the wine of the wrath of her fornication, that persecuteth the saints of God, that shed their blood—she who sitteth upon many waters, and upon the islands of the sea—behold, she is the tares of the earth; she is bound in bundles; her bands are made strong, no man can loose them; therefore, she is ready to be burned. And he shall sound his trump both long and loud, and all nations shall hear it" (D&C 88:94).

An angel's trump announces, "It is finished"

"And again, another angel shall sound his trump, which is the seventh angel, saying: It is finished; it is finished! The Lamb of God hath overcome and trodden the wine-press alone, even the wine-press of the fierceness of the wrath of Almighty God" (D&C 88:106).

ANGELS ANNOUNCE THE SECOND COMING WITH THE SOUND OF A TRUMP

"Angels shall fly through the midst of heaven, crying with a loud voice, sounding the trump of God, saying . . . Behold, and lo, the Bridegroom cometh; go ye out to meet him" (D&C 88:92). Paul taught that Michael the archangel would announce Christ's descent from heaven: "The Lord himself shall descend from heaven with a shout, with the voice of the archangel, and with the trump of God" (1 Thessalonians 4:16). And a latter-day revelation states, "For behold, the Lord God hath sent forth the angel crying through the midst of heaven, saying: Prepare ye the way of the Lord, and make his paths straight, for the hour of his coming is nigh" (D&C 133:17).

ANGELS WILL ACCOMPANY JESUS AT HIS SECOND COMING

The apostle Paul wrote, "The Lord Jesus shall be revealed from heaven with his mighty angels, in flaming fire taking vengeance on them that know not God, and that obey not the gospel of our Lord Jesus Christ" (2 Thessalonians 1:7–8). Jesus himself said: "Blessed is he who cometh in the name of the Lord, in the clouds of heaven, and all the holy angels with him. Then understood his disciples that he should come again on the earth, after that he was glorified and crowned on the right hand of God" (Joseph Smith–Matthew 1:1). And further, the Lord revealed to Joseph Smith, "And then they shall look for me, and, behold, I will come; and they shall see me in the clouds of heaven, clothed with power and great glory; with all the holy angels" (D&C 45:44). An additional witness states that "the Son of man shall come in the glory of his Father with his angels" (Matthew 16:27).

ANGELS DO NOT KNOW THE HOUR OR THE DAY OF THE SECOND COMING

Although angels have prominent roles during the last days and at the Second Coming, they do not know the hour or the day of his coming. Days before his death on the cross, Jesus spoke privately to his disciples while sitting on the Mount of Olives. Jesus gave them signs by which they would know that his coming was "near, even at the doors" (Joseph Smith–Matthew 1:39). Then he said, "But of that day, and hour, no one knoweth; no, not the angels of God in heaven, but my Father only" (Joseph Smith–Matthew 1:40). The triple negative ("no one knoweth; no, not") emphasizes that even the angels do not know the time of his coming.

Statements similar to one spoken by Jesus on the Mount of Olives were also revealed to Joseph Smith, in somewhat different words: "which time is nigh at hand—I, the Lord God, have spoken it; but the hour and the day no man knoweth, neither the angels in heaven, nor shall they know until he comes" (D&C 49:6–7; see also 39:21). God, in his infinite wisdom and knowledge, has not shared with his angels his knowledge about the time of Christ's second coming.

Chapter 30

CHARIOTS AND
HORSES OF FIRE

*Like that servant of Elisha, there are more with
you than those you can see opposed to you. Some who
are with you will be invisible to your mortal eyes.*

PRESIDENT HENRY B. EYRING

When we read of angels and chariots and horses of fire, we must remain tentative because we do not always know when the chariots and horses of fire are literal, when they are symbolic, or when they are both literal and symbolic. Consider, for example, a passage from Isaiah that depicts the Lord coming with chariots: "For, behold, the Lord will come with fire, and with his chariots like a whirlwind, to render his anger with fury, and his rebuke with flames of fire" (Isaiah 66:15). Additionally, we must remember that accounts of chariots and horses of fire are quite rare. Angels are not usually associated with chariots, but we know that chariots and horses of fire, attested in both in the Old Testament and in our own dispensation, provide protection to God's covenant people.

"O Ye That Embark," *Ensign*, Nov. 2008, 58.

ELIJAH AND A CHARIOT OF FIRE AND HORSES OF FIRE

Shortly before the prophet Elijah was translated and taken up into heaven by a whirlwind, he traveled with Elisha to the Jordan River. After crossing the Jordan, as Elijah and Elisha were walking and talking, "there appeared a chariot of fire, and horses of fire, and parted them both asunder; and Elijah went up by a whirlwind into heaven." When Elisha witnessed this scene, he cried out, "My father, my father, the chariot of Israel, and the horsemen thereof" (2 Kings 2:11–12; see also 2 Kings 13:14). A chariot of fire, horses of fire, and Elijah ascending to heaven in a whirlwind create a magnificent and marvelous show of power.

ELISHA AND CHARIOTS OF FIRE

Sometime later, as Israel's prophet, Elisha had another experience with chariots and horses of fire. Syria's king, attempting to capture Elisha in the city of Dothan, surrounded Dothan with soldiers, horses, and chariots. When Elisha's servant awakened early in the morning, he saw the armies that surrounded the city and cried out to Elisha, "Alas, my master! how shall we do?" Elisha replied, "Fear not: for they that be with us are more than they that be with them." And this truly was the case, for "Elisha prayed, and said, Lord, I pray thee, open his eyes, that he may see. And the Lord opened the eyes of the young man; and he saw: and, behold, the mountain was full of horses and chariots of fire round about Elisha" (2 Kings 6:15–17). Beyond doubt, as the psalmist wrote, "The chariots of God are twenty thousand, even thousands upon thousands; The Lord is among them, as in Sinai, in the sanctuary" (ASV, Psalm 68:17).

Our general authorities have likened the account of Elisha

and his servant to us. Elder Jeffrey R. Holland gave us this wonderful promise: "In the gospel of Jesus Christ we have help from both sides of the veil. When disappointment and discouragement strike—and they will—we need to remember that if our eyes could be opened, we would see horses and chariots of fire as far as the eye can see, riding at great speed to come to our protection. They will always be there, these armies of heaven, in defense of Abraham's seed."[1]

President Henry B. Eyring encouraged us: "I know that the promise of angels to bear us up is real. You might want to bring to memory the assurance of Elisha to his frightened servant. That assurance is ours when we feel close to being overwhelmed in our service. Elisha faced real and terrible opposition. . . . Like that servant of Elisha, there are more with you than those you can see opposed to you. Some who are with you will be invisible to your mortal eyes."[2]

THE PROPHET ZECHARIAH SEES FOUR CHARIOTS IN VISION

Zechariah received a vision of four chariots with horses (Zechariah 6:1–3). Afterward, Zechariah inquired of the heavenly messenger who was helping him to understand the vision: "What are these, my lord? And the angel answered and said unto me, These are the four spirits of the heavens, which go forth from standing before the Lord of all the earth" (Zechariah 6:4–5). The four spirits are four angels that move to and fro upon the earth

---

1. *However Long and Hard the Road*, 13–14.
2. "O Ye That Embark," *Ensign*, Nov. 2008, 58.

in God's service (see Hebrews 1:7, 14). The chariots represent the angels' ability to move about as they serve God.

Chariots and horses of fire in the Kirtland Temple

During the season of preparation leading up to the dedication of the Kirtland Temple, some of the Saints saw marvelous, sacred things—chariots of Israel, an angel riding a horse of fire, the armies of heaven, and other manifestations of great significance. The following account of events on January 28, 1836, is unmistakably clear that the angels who encircled the temple did so to protect the Saints from Satan's host of evil spirits: "Elder Roger Orton saw a mighty angel riding upon a horse of fire, with a flaming sword in his hand, followed by five others, encircle the house, and protect the Saints, even the Lord's anointed, from the power of Satan and a host of evil spirits, which were striving to disturb the Saints. President William Smith, one of the Twelve, saw the heavens opened, and the Lord's host protecting the Lord's anointed."[3] This account does not give the identity of the "mighty angel riding upon a horse of fire," but note that the expression "mighty angel" is also used in the book of Revelation (10:1; 18:1).

Harrison Burgess, who attended the dedication of the Kirtland Temple, recorded the following about events on March 30, 1836: "The Spirit of God rested upon me in mighty power. . . . I beheld the Prophet Joseph and Hyrum Smith and Roger Orton enveloped in the light: Joseph exclaimed aloud, 'I behold the Savior, the Son of God.' Hyrum said, 'I behold the angels of heaven.' Brother Orton exclaimed, 'I behold the chariots of

---

3. Smith, *History of the Church*, 2:386–87; paragraphing altered.

Israel.' All who were in the room felt the power of God to that degree that many prophesied, and the power of God was made manifest, the remembrance of which will remain with me while I live upon the earth."[4]

Others also saw the chariots of Israel. The Prophet Joseph Smith recorded: "The heavens were opened unto Elder Sylvester Smith, and he, leaping up, exclaimed: 'The horsemen of Israel and the chariots thereof.'"[5]

Benjamin Brown likewise recorded that some individuals saw angels and chariots: "Some have seen the heavens opend & seen the [S]avior others have seen angels on the four corners of the house of the Lord with drawn swords & also stood thick on the ridge Elisha with his chariot of Fire, Peter John & James, & the highway cast up the ten tribes returning in chariots as far as the eye could extend some saw the Redemption of Zion. . . . Father Stephens saw on Sunday evening two rows of Angels through the House, at another time the glory of God came down on the Elders from the head down half way—April 29th an angel was seen over the Elders . . . the Heavens was opened two saw the Savior some saw chariots."[6]

Three of Brother Brown's statements are particularly noteworthy in connection with chariots. First, he stated that when heaven was opened, some of the worshippers saw "Elisha with his chariot of fire." Second, he stated that a number of people also saw in

---

4. "Sketch of a Well-Spent Life," 67.

5. *History of the Church*, 2:383.

6. Harper, "Pentecost and Endowment Indeed," in Welch and Carlson, *Opening the Heavens*, 335, 337.

vision the return of the ten tribes on the highway that would be cast up and writes that they were "returning in chariots as far as the eye could extend." Third, he added that "some saw chariots."

Elder Erastus Snow provided additional information about chariots when he wrote that some of the Saints "saw Zion in her glory & the angels came & worshipped with us & some saw them, yea, even twelve legions of them, the charriots of Israel and the horsemen thereof."[7] Joseph Smith's scribe saw "armies of heaven" (perhaps including chariots?) protecting the Saints as they were returning to Zion.[8]

---

7. "Sketch Book," 6.
8. *History of the Church*, 2:381.

Chapter 31

ANGELS WITH DRAWN SWORDS IN THEIR HANDS

Elder Roger Orton saw a mighty angel riding upon a horse of fire, with a flaming sword in his hand.

JOSEPH SMITH

A few ancient and modern accounts portray angels with swords in their hands. When we discuss angels and swords, we must keep an open mind because it is often difficult to determine when angels' swords in such accounts are purely symbolic, when they are literal, or when they are both.

At times an angel's sword is designed to protect the righteous, but at other times it is meant to destroy the wicked. The following accounts set forth examples of both the sword that protects and the sword that destroys. An episode in the life of King David pertains to his committing a sin that displeased God so greatly that he would smite Israel (see 1 Chronicles 21:1–30). But in His mercy, God allowed David to choose from three forms of punishment—three years of famine, three months of destruction by one of Israel's enemies, "or else three days the sword of the Lord, even

---

History of the Church, 2:386–87.

215

the pestilence, in the land, and the angel of the Lord destroying throughout all the coasts of Israel" (1 Chronicles 21:10–12). David chose three days of the angel's sword, hoping that the Lord would have greater mercy than Israel's enemies (see 1 Chronicles 21:13). The chronicler explains that the angel's sword in this case signified a pestilence (see 1 Chronicles 21:12, 14).

The narrative continues: "David lifted up his eyes, and saw the angel of the Lord stand between the earth and the heaven, having a drawn sword in his hand stretched out over Jerusalem" (1 Chronicles 21:16). At one point, the Lord's angel counseled David through Gad that if David would build an altar and offer sacrifices to the Lord, then the plague would end. David followed the seer's counsel, so "the Lord commanded the angel; and he put up his sword again into the sheath thereof" (1 Chronicles 21:27).

An intriguing account in Numbers 22 features three chief participants: an angel with a drawn sword in his hand, the man named Balaam, and a beast that discerned the presence of the angel. The text refers to "the angel of the Lord standing in the way, and his sword drawn in his hand. . . . Then the Lord opened the eyes of Balaam, and he saw the angel of the Lord standing in the way, and his sword drawn in his hand" (Numbers 22:23–31). We may draw from this true story many levels of understanding; that the angel had a drawn sword in his hand is particularly significant.

A well-known narrative regarding angels with swords is that of the cherubim in the Garden of Eden. Genesis 3:24 states that the Lord God "drove out the man; and he stationed at the east of the garden of Eden cherubim, and a flaming, revolving sword, to guard the path of the tree of life" (translation mine). Three features included in the phrase "a flaming, revolving sword" combine to inspire fear in potential intruders. The first feature is the sword itself. With rare exceptions, the sword in the Old Testament refers to a weapon of war or an instrument of destruction (Numbers 19:16; Joshua 10:11; 13:22; 1 Samuel 7:51).

The second feature is the flame of fire ("flaming"). The fire makes the sword under discussion exceptional: In addition to the danger of the blade itself, this sword could burn or scorch as it slashed and cut. A verse from Isaiah also connects *fire* and *sword:* "For by fire and by his sword will the Lord plead with all flesh: and the slain of the Lord shall be many" (Isaiah 66:16; see also vv. 15, 17).

The third feature that may cause dread is expressed by the Hebrew verb *hamithapeket,* which translates into the English term "revolving" or "turned every way," as used in the King James Version. This verb makes it clear that the sword is continually whirling or revolving, perhaps in a zigzagging manner, to protect the path to the tree of life. It would be difficult or impossible for unauthorized individuals to proceed past such a revolving sword.

The flaming sword of Genesis has a parallel in the remarkable spiritual events that occurred in the evening of January 28, 1836, during the season of the dedication of the Kirtland Temple. As we have noted, Joseph Smith recorded that Elder Roger Orton beheld angels with flaming swords protecting the Lord's Saints from Satan and his evil ones.[1]

---

1. *History of the Church,* 2:386–87.

The Prophet Joseph also saw an angel with a drawn sword protecting Brigham Young while he was in an adverse situation. Joseph recorded that he envisioned "Elder Brigham Young standing in a strange land, in the far south and west, in a desert place, upon a rock in the midst of about a dozen men . . . who, appeared hostile. He was preaching to them in their own tongue, and the angel of God standing above his head, with a drawn sword in his hand, protecting him, but he did not see it."[2]

Again, the swords of these angels are probably symbolic, as in the following scriptural passages that state that the Lord himself has a sword: "Happy art thou, O Israel: who is like unto thee, O people saved by the Lord, the shield of thy help, and who is the sword of thy excellency!" (Deuteronomy 33:29); "the Lord with his sore and great and strong sword" (Isaiah 27:1); "The sword of the Lord" (Isaiah 34:6; see also Jeremiah 12:12); "O thou sword of the Lord" (Jeremiah 47:6); "I the Lord have drawn forth my sword out of his sheath" (Ezekiel 21:5).

Symbolically, the Lord's sword executes judgment and destruction upon Earth's inhabitants, but the sword also signifies the Lord's ability to protect his people from spiritual and mortal danger. Protection of his people seems to have been the purpose of the sword when the Lord appeared to Joshua.[3] "And it came to pass, when Joshua was by Jericho, that he lifted up his eyes and looked, and, behold, there stood a man over against him with his sword drawn in his hand: and Joshua went unto him, and said

---

2. *History of the Church,* 2:381.

3. Biblical commentators generally concur that the being who appeared to Joshua was none other than the Lord.

unto him, Art thou for us, or for our adversaries? And he said, Nay; but as captain of the host of the Lord am I now come. And Joshua fell on his face to the earth, and did worship, and said unto him, What saith my lord unto his servant? And the captain of the Lord's host said unto Joshua, Loose thy shoe from off thy foot; for the place whereon thou standest is holy. And Joshua did so" (Joshua 5:13–15; cf. Exodus 3:5).

At first Joshua did not recognize the Lord, so Joshua asked him if he was Israel's friend or foe. After the Lord assured Joshua that he, Jehovah, was in fact the captain of Israel's army, Joshua recognized him and worshipped him. The sword referred to in Joshua 5:13–15 denotes Jehovah's power to protect Israel as it went forth to fulfill God's command to conquer its enemies. In the end, Joshua and Israel conquered thirty-one kings together with their kingdoms (Joshua 12:20). How could an untrained army complete such an undertaking? Joshua 10:42 concludes that "all these kings and their land did Joshua take at one time, because the Lord God of Israel fought for Israel" (Joshua 10:42).

Chapter 32

ANGELS WITH KEYS
IN THEIR HANDS

*When Peter came and sat in the Temple in
Kirtland, he . . . had a key in his hand.*

PRESIDENT HEBER C. KIMBALL

Rarely is an angel represented as having a key in his hand. When he visited the Kirtland Temple, Peter held a key, which may symbolize authority from God. President Thomas S. Monson wrote of the "keys of the ministering angels" and the "keys of the Melchizedek Priesthood," connecting these keys to "divine authority": "John the Baptist, on May 15, 1829, . . . laid his hands upon Joseph Smith and Oliver Cowdery and ordained them, saying, 'Upon you my fellow servants, in the name of Messiah I confer the Priesthood of Aaron, which holds the keys of the ministering of angels' . . . The messenger announced that he acted under the direction of Peter, James, and John, who held the keys of the Melchizedek Priesthood. Ordination and baptism followed. This is yet another example of divine authority by direct revelation."[1]

Journal of Discourses, 9:376.

1. "Our Sacred Priesthood Trust," *Ensign,* May 2006, 55.

THE KEY IN PETER'S HAND

In the Tabernacle in Salt Lake City, on February 9, 1862, President Heber C. Kimball spoke of seeing the apostle Peter years earlier in the Kirtland Temple: "Let me inform you that when Peter came and sat in the Temple in Kirtland, he had on a neat woolen garment, nicely adjusted round the neck . . . and he also had a key in his hand." President Kimball suggested that Peter's key signified his priesthood authority: "John [the Baptist] also came and administered unto Joseph Smith, and remember that Peter, James and John hold the keys pertaining to their dispensation and pertaining to this, and they came and conferred their Priesthood and authority upon Joseph the Seer, which is for the gathering together of all who seek the way of life."[2]

Elder Erastus Snow recalled that at the Kirtland Temple dedication in 1836, "Peter, James, and John and Elijah [were] Seen in the Holy of Holies with golden keys in their hands, in the Arch of the Temple."[3] At the same dedication, Benjamin Brown wrote that one of the worshippers "saw a pillow or cloud rest down upon the house bright as when the sun shines on a cloud like as gold, two others saw three personages hovering in the room with bright keys in their hands."[4]

AN ANGEL WITH THE KEY TO THE BOTTOMLESS PIT

In Joseph Smith's translation of Revelation 9:1, an angel is

---

2. *Journal of Discourses,* 9:376.
3. Cited in *Diary of Charles Lowell Walker,* 2:563; see also Brown and Smith, *Symbols in Stone,* 58.
4. Harper, "Pentecost and Endowment Indeed," in Welch and Carlson, *Opening the Heavens,* 336.

given the key to the bottomless pit. In Revelation 20:1, that angel goes from heaven with the key to capture the devil and throw him into a bottomless pit, where he must remain for a thousand years. John recorded: "And I saw an angel come down from heaven, having the key of the bottomless pit and a great chain in his hand. And he laid hold on the dragon, that old serpent, which is the Devil, and Satan, and bound him a thousand years, and cast him into the bottomless pit, and shut him up, and set a seal upon him, that he should deceive the nations no more, till the thousand years should be fulfilled" (Revelation 20:1–3). The "great chain" in the angel's hands tells us that not only will the devil be cast into prison but a chain will bind him there, evoking shackles and emphasizing that there is no hope of his escape. We do not know the identity of this angel, but obviously it is a being of great power.

WILFORD WOODRUFF RECEIVES KEYS OF THE TEMPLE

President Wilford Woodruff recorded: "Near fifty years ago while in the city of Boston I had a vision of going with the Saints to the Rocky Mountains building a temple and I dedicated it. Two nights in succession before John Taylor's death President Brigham Young [who had died many years earlier] gave me the keys of the temple and told me to go and dedicate it, which I did."[5]

---

5. Journal, Dec. 31, 1893.

Chapter 33

ANGELS WITH TRUMPETS HERALD GREAT EVENTS

❧❦

O that I were an angel . . . that I might go
forth and speak with the trump of God.

ALMA 29:1

In the last days a few angels will sound trumpets to herald the everlasting gospel, to invite people to repent, to gather the elect, to make specific announcements, to warn of impending danger or coming judgments, to announce the resurrection, and to proclaim the second coming of Jesus Christ. Whether people on earth will actually hear these trumpets, and whether the trumpets are literal or symbolic or both, has not yet been revealed.

The following are accounts of angels with trumpets.

SEVEN ANGELS PREPARE TO SOUND THEIR TRUMPETS

As recorded in Revelation 8:1–5, several events occur in the temple in heaven when Christ opens the seventh and final seal. John witnesses that the seven angels receive seven trumpets. In verse 6 he sees them prepare to blow their trumpets, and in verse 7 the first angel blows his trumpet. The chief goal of these angels is to prepare for the second coming of Christ: "The sounding of the trumpets of the seven angels are the preparing and finishing of [God's] work . . . the preparing of the way before the time of [Christ's] coming" (D&C 77:12). This sounding of trumpets will occur "in the beginning of the seventh thousand years" (D&C 77:12).

These seven angels may be the same seven angels identified in Revelation 15:1, 6–8; 16:1, who pour out seven plagues upon the earth's inhabitants. Apocryphal sources name the seven angels as Uriel, Raphael, Raguel, Michael, Saraqael, Gabriel, and Remiel (1 Enoch 20:1–8). All of these names end in the particle *el*, which means "God." One source depicts one angel stating, "I am Raphael, one of the seven holy angels which present the prayers of the saints, and which go in and out before the Holy One" (Tobit 12:15). Luke 1:19 records, "I am Gabriel, that stand in the presence of God," and we know of Michael, Gabriel, and Raphael from modern-day revelation (D&C 128:21).

Great destructions occur upon the earth at the sounding of each trump. For instance, as the first angel sounds his trump, "there followed hail and fire mingled with blood, and they were cast upon the earth: and the third part of trees was burnt up, and all green grass was burnt up" (Revelation 8:7).

Besides these seven angels, other angels will also herald significant events:

ANGELS HERALD THE EVERLASTING GOSPEL

Revelation 14:6 reads, "And I saw another angel fly in the midst of heaven, having the everlasting gospel to preach unto them that dwell on the earth, and to every nation, and kindred, and tongue, and people." The Prophet Joseph Smith said of this angel, "John saw the angel having the holy Priesthood, who should preach the everlasting Gospel to all nations. God had an angel—a special messenger—ordained and prepared for that purpose in the last days."[1] This angel is apparently the same one who will sound the fifth trump at the time of the resurrection and the end of the world (see D&C 88:94–110; 133:36–40).

This angel may be the angel that President John Taylor saw in vision as a child. Elder B. H. Roberts wrote of President Taylor: "When but a small boy he saw, in vision, an angel in the heavens, holding a trumpet to his mouth, sounding a message to the nations. The import of this vision he did not understand until later in life."[2]

ANGELS WITH TRUMPETS INVITE PEOPLE TO REPENT

Alma exclaimed, "O that I were an angel, and could have the wish of mine heart, that I might go forth and speak with the trump of God, with a voice to shake the earth, and cry repentance unto every people!" (Alma 29:1). In another passage, the Lord gives methods by which he encourages people to repent, including "the ministering of angels" as well as "the great sound of a trump," presumably blown by an angel (D&C 43:25).

ANGELS WITH TRUMPETS GATHER THE ELECT

The Lord sends angels to assist in the gathering of his elect. "The Son of Man shall come, and he shall send his angels before him with the great sound of a trumpet, and they shall gather

---

1. *Teachings of the Prophet Joseph Smith*, 365.
2. *Life of John Taylor*, 28.

together the remainder of his elect from the four winds, from one end of heaven to the other" (Joseph Smith–Matthew 1:37).

ANGELS ANNOUNCE GOD'S JUDGMENTS AND CALAMITIES

God has commissioned some of his angels to have authority over particular calamities, catastrophes, and disasters in the last days. These calamities, catastrophes, and disasters, which are directed to the wicked, are collectively called God's judgments and include such devastations as earthquakes, tornadoes, famines, wars, pestilences, scourges, plagues, tsunamis, hail, storms, whirlwinds, hurricanes, and much more.

AN ANGEL'S TRUMP ANNOUNCES THE BURNING OF "THAT GREAT CHURCH, THE MOTHER OF ABOMINATIONS"

"And another angel shall sound his trump, saying: That great church, the mother of abominations, that made all nations drink of the wine of the wrath of her fornication, that persecuteth the saints of God . . . she is ready to be burned. And he shall sound his trump both long and loud, and all nations shall hear it" (D&C 88:94). An angel—perhaps the same one—shall also sound the trump after the fall of this church: "And again, another angel shall sound his trump, which is the sixth angel, saying: She is fallen who made all nations drink of the wine of the wrath of her fornication; she is fallen, is fallen!" (D&C 88:105).

AN ANGEL'S TRUMP ANNOUNCES, "IT IS FINISHED"

"And again, another angel shall sound his trump, which is the seventh angel, saying: It is finished; it is finished! The Lamb of God hath overcome and trodden the wine-press alone, even the wine-press of the fierceness of the wrath of Almighty God" (D&C 88:106).

AN ANGEL WITH A TRUMPET ANNOUNCES THE LORD'S COMING

The apostle Paul taught that Michael the archangel would announce Christ's descent from heaven: "The Lord himself shall descend from heaven with a shout, with the voice of the archangel, and with the trump of God" (1 Thessalonians 4:16).

ANGELS WITH TRUMPETS ANNOUNCE THE RESURRECTION

God has prepared four angels to sound their trumpets to announce the resurrection that is yet to come. Each will blow his trump in his own turn (D&C 88:97–102). The sounding of the first trumpet awakens those who lived a celestial law. The sounding of the next three trumpets awakens those who lived a terrestrial law, followed by those who lived a telestial law, and finally those "who shall remain filthy still" (D&C 88:102; see also 1 Thessalonians 4:16–17; D&C 45:45).

SEVEN ANGELS' TRUMPS REVEAL MEN'S "SECRET ACTS" AND GOD'S "MIGHTY WORKS"

"And then shall the first angel again sound his trump in the ears of all living, and reveal the secret acts of men, and the mighty works of God in the first thousand years. And then shall the second angel sound his trump, and reveal the secret acts of men, and the thoughts and intents of their hearts, and the mighty works of God in the second thousand years—and so on, until the seventh angel shall sound his trump" (D&C 88:108–10).

Conclusion

ANGELS MINISTER AMONG US TODAY

❧❧❧

*In times of special need, He sent angels,
divine messengers, to bless His children, reassure
them that heaven was always very close and
that His help was always very near.*

ELDER JEFFREY R. HOLLAND

Some of the accounts of angels contained in this book are exceptional or unique, for example, angels and chariots and angels with swords in their hands. Most of us will never be protected by an angel in a lion's den nor be privileged to see horses and chariots of fire. But most of the accounts of angels discussed in this book pertain to ordinary men, women, and children. We should bear in mind that angelic communications are not reserved for those who lived during the ancient periods of the Old Testament or Book of Mormon, nor are such communications reserved only for prophets, apostles, or notable women, such as Hagar or Mary, the mother of Jesus. Indeed, several of the general authorities of the Church have clearly taught that anyone may receive angelic communications, according to the divine will of our loving Heavenly Father.

"The Ministry of Angels," *Ensign*, Nov. 2008, 29.

Angelic activities in this dispensation have greatly affected me; in truth, they have affected each one who partakes of the blessings of the gospel in this dispensation. Because of the work of angels, we are able to enjoy the gifts and blessings of the ordinances, such as those of baptism, the sacrament, and the temple (see chapter 16). It is difficult to imagine the gospel without the sacrament, which is vital to the plan of salvation as we seek to repent and obtain forgiveness of our sins during mortality. But because of angels, we may enjoy the gift of the sacrament on a weekly basis. Also, the power and authority to baptize were restored by an angel, as were the temple ordinances that link families together in eternal units. Angels restored to the Prophet Joseph Smith the power and authority to perform these and other ordinances.

Moreover, an angel revealed the marvelous Book of Mormon, the keystone of our religion. When we faithfully study its contents, this sacred book draws us closer to God, makes us more spiritually attuned, prepares us to receive revelation, makes us better husbands, wives, and children, and protects us from the forces of evil. This Christ-centered book of scripture draws us closer to our Savior and Redeemer. It is difficult to imagine our religion without the Book of Mormon, which Moroni revealed to Joseph Smith.

Beyond the gospel ordinances and the gift of the Book of Mormon, angels affect each one of us in many other ways (see chapters 10–29 in this volume). During the last days, for example, angels are inviting people to repent. In this capacity, they are co-workers with our full- and part-time missionaries. Angels are also assisting in the gathering of the elect from all nations. Furthermore, God has commissioned some of his angels to have authority over particular calamities, catastrophes, and disasters in the last days. These events are directed to the wicked to invite them to repent. Angels have yet another crucial responsibility—to accompany Jesus at his second coming.

It is my understanding, based on more than twenty years of study and research, that the ministrations of angels are largely unknown to mortals. Angels move about the earth conducting the Lord's divine work. They serve, minister, and mingle among us, usually without our awareness. Most of us in mortality will never see an angel, but each of us nevertheless enjoys the blessings of the restored gospel because of the divinely directed actions of angels.

All the Lord's angels minister with heavenly love, and every angelic communication is a message of love. We may say without any hesitation that angels are agents of love, and they are also agents of great power. They possess extraordinary capabilities and faculties, making them formidable beings. And they are agents of light because of their righteousness and goodness. Ultimately, their love and power and light exist because of the atonement of Jesus Christ, who enlightens all who love him and keep his commandments.

I believe with Elder Jeffrey R. Holland that "we need to speak of and believe in and bear testimony of the ministry of angels more than we sometimes do."[1] I bear testimony that angels are agents of love, light, and power. They exist because of Jesus Christ and his infinite atonement. Angels appeared to the Prophet Joseph Smith, and I testify that the sacred work of angels continues in our day.

---

1. "For a Wise Purpose," *Ensign*, Jan. 1996, 17.

SIGNERS OF THE DECLARATION OF INDEPENDENCE AND OTHER EMINENT PERSONS

In August 1877, while President Wilford Woodruff was serving as president of the St. George Temple, a number of eminent men who were disembodied spirits ministered to, or "waited on," President Woodruff "for two days and two nights."[1] These men included George Washington, John Adams, Thomas Jefferson, Benjamin Franklin, other members of the Continental Congress who signed the Declaration of Independence, and more. The great historical significance of these men and their contributions to the founding of the United States cannot be assessed too highly, and their appearing to an apostle of the Lord is momentous to the history of the LDS Church and to the understanding of the operations of angels. President Ezra Taft Benson affirmed, "The temple work for the fifty-six signers of the Declaration of Independence and other Founding Fathers has been done. All these appeared to Wilford Woodruff when he was president of the St. George Temple."[2]

Different sources record the visitations of these eminent men. First and foremost are the words of President Woodruff. Less than a month after these men visited him, he stated:

"Two weeks before I left St. George, the spirits of the dead gathered around me, wanting to know why we did not redeem them. Said they, 'you have had the use of the Endowment House for a number of years, and yet nothing has ever been done for us. We laid the foundation

---

1. *Journal of Discourses*, 19:229; see also chapter 1 of this volume.
2. *Teachings of Ezra Taft Benson*, 604.

of the government you now enjoy, and we never apostatized from it, but we remained true to it and were faithful to God.' These were the signers of the Declaration of Independence, and they waited on me for two days and two nights. I thought it very singular, that notwithstanding so much work had been done, and yet nothing had been done for them. The thought never entered my heart, from the fact, I suppose, that heretofore our minds were reaching after our more immediate friends and relatives. I straightway went into the baptismal font and called upon brother McCallister to baptize me for the signers of the Declaration of Independence, and fifty other eminent men, making one hundred in all, including John Wesley, Columbus, and others; I then baptized him for every President of the United States, except three; and when their cause is just, somebody will do the work for them."[3]

These visitations took place two weeks before he left St. George in 1877. His journal records that he left St. George on August 30 to attend President Brigham Young's funeral in Salt Lake City. These facts point to the Signers and others appearing to President Woodruff about August 16. That conclusion is supported by his journal entry of Sunday, August 19: "I spent the Evening in preparing a list of the Noted Men of the 17 Centaury and 18th including the signers of the declaration of Independance, and the Presidents of the United States, for Baptism on Tuesday the 21 Aug 1877."[4]

The Signers explained to President Woodruff, "We laid the foundation of the government you now enjoy, and we never apostatized from it, but we remained true to it." The Founding Fathers fought battles and wars, and they wrote and signed documents that would have far-reaching historical and political significance for generations. In short, they wore out their lives in establishing the nation that would become the cradle of the restoration of the gospel of Jesus Christ.

And yet, in the centuries since their day, some have called into question the character, motives, spirituality, or morality of the

---

3. *Journal of Discourses,* 19:229.
4. Journal, Aug. 19, 1896.

Founding Fathers. But note President Benson's words: "When one casts doubt about the character of these noble sons of God, I believe he or she will have to answer to the God of heaven for it."[5] As a matter of fact, President Benson, time and time again, taught that the Founding Fathers were God-fearing men who were often led by divine inspiration: "After he became President of the Church, President Wilford Woodruff declared that 'those men who laid the foundation of this American government were the best spirits the God of heaven could find on the face of the earth. They were choice spirits [and] were inspired of the Lord.'"[6]

President Woodruff said, "These were the signers of the Declaration of Independence, and they waited on me for two days and two nights." The visitation of these men was not a brief one, nor did the men appear in an ordinary dream. President Benson stated that "the Founding Fathers . . . did appear to Wilford Woodruff twice and asked why the work hadn't been done for them. They had founded this country and the Constitution of this land, and they had been true to those principles."[7] President Woodruff "straightway went into the baptismal font" to be baptized on behalf of all the signers of the Declaration of Independence, except William Floyd and John Hancock; he did not record an explanation for those two exceptions.

Following, in alphabetical order by surname, are the names of a number of the Signers, together with brief biographical information. The name of the colony each represented at the Continental Congress is included.[8]

John Adams (Massachusetts, 1735–1826). First vice president of the United States under George Washington and second president of the United States.

Samuel Adams (Massachusetts, 1722–1803). Governor of Massachusetts.

---

5. *Teachings of Ezra Taft Benson*, 604.
6. *Teachings of Ezra Taft Benson*, 598–605.
7. *Teachings of Ezra Taft Benson*, 604.
8. I appreciate Jared Pfost for assisting in researching and gathering biographical information from various encyclopedias and Internet sources for this appendix.

APPENDIX

Josiah Bartlett (New Hampshire, 1729–1795). Judge; president (governor) of New Hampshire.

Carter Braxton (Virginia, 1736–1797). American statesman.

Charles Carroll (Virginia, 1737–1832). Virginia state senator and later U.S. senator.

Samuel Chase (Maryland, 1741–1811). Appointed an associate justice of the Supreme Court by George Washington.

Abraham Clark (New Jersey, 1726–1794). Political leader who defended poor farmers.

George Clymer (Pennsylvania, 1739–1813). Merchant and politician; founded the Philadelphia Academy of Fine Arts and the Philadelphia Bank.

William Ellery (Rhode Island, 1727–1820). Collector of customs.

Benjamin Franklin (Pennsylvania, 1706–1790). Printer; publisher; civic leader; statesman; scientist; inventor; patriot.

Elbridge Gerry (Massachusetts, 1744–1814). Governor of Massachusetts; vice president of the United States under President James Madison.

Button Gwinnett (Georgia, 1735?–1777). Acting governor of Georgia for a time in 1777; killed in a duel.

Lyman Hall (Georgia, 1724–1790). Studied for the ministry; later became a doctor and governor of Georgia.

Benjamin Harrison (Virginia, 1726?–1791). Presided over debates in the Continental Congress while the Declaration of Independence was formulated; son William Henry Harrison and great-grandson Benjamin Harrison each became president of the United States.

John Hart (New Jersey, 1711?–1779). Farmer; patriot.

Joseph Hewes (North Carolina, 1730–1779). Head of the Continental Navy; provided John Paul Jones with a ship and appointed him an officer.

Thomas Heywood Jr. (South Carolina, 1746–1809). Soldier; judge; statesman.

William Hooper (North Carolina, 1742–1790). Studied law.

Stephen Hopkins (Rhode Island, 1707–1785). Statesman; judge; governor.

Francis Hopkinson (New Jersey, 1737–1791). Writer; artist; judge; lawyer; likely the designer of the flag of the United States.

Samuel Huntington (Connecticut, 1731–1796). Chief justice of Connecticut; governor of Connecticut.

Thomas Jefferson (Virginia, 1743–1826). Inventor; architect; statesman;

author of the Declaration of Independence; governor of Virginia; vice president and then president of the United States.

Francis Lightfoot Lee (Virginia, 1734–1797). Plantation owner; protester against the British Stamp Act and other acts.

Richard Henry Lee (Virginia, 1732–1794). President of Continental Congress; protester against the British Stamp Act and other acts.

Francis Lewis (New York, 1713–1802). Patriot; spent much of his fortune in support of the Americans in the Revolutionary War.

Philip Livingston (New York, 1716–1778). Importer and statesman; spent much of his fortune in support of the Americans in the Revolutionary War.

Thomas Lynch Jr. (South Carolina, 1749–1779). Served in the Revolutionary War; lost at sea in 1779.

Thomas McKean (Delaware, 1734–1817). Chief justice of Delaware; governor of Delaware.

Lewis Morris (New York, 1726–1798). Fought in the Revolutionary War.

Robert Morris (Pennsylvania, 1735–1806). Signer of both the Declaration of Independence and the Constitution of the United States; raised so much money to support the Continental Army that he was called "the financier of the American Revolution."

John Morton (Pennsylvania, 1724–1777). Surveyor; judge.

Arthur Myddleton, or *Middleton* (South Carolina, 1742–1787). Served in the Revolutionary War.

Thomas Nelson Jr. (Virginia, 1738–1789). Served in the Revolutionary War; governor of Virginia.

William Chase Paca (Maryland, 1740–1799). Governor of Maryland; judge.

Robert Treat Paine (Maine, 1731–1814). Statesman; attorney general; judge; cofounder of American Academy of Arts and Sciences.

John Penn (North Carolina, 1740–1788). Lawyer.

George Read (Delaware, 1733–1798). Lawyer; state attorney general; signer of both the Declaration of Independence and the Constitution.

Caezar Rodney (Delaware, 1728–1784). President (governor) of Delaware.

George Ross (Pennsylvania, 1730–1779). Lawyer; judge.

Benjamin Rush (Pennsylvania, 1745–1813). Physician; surgeon general in the Continental Army; treasurer of the U.S. Mint.

Edward Rutledge (South Carolina, 1749–1800). Statesman; lawyer; governor of South Carolina.

Roger Sherman (Connecticut, 1721–1793). Statesman; businessman; judge;

the only man to sign all four founding documents of the United States: Articles of Association (1774), Declaration of Independence (1776), Articles of Confederation (1777), and Constitution of the United States (1787).

James Smith (Pennsylvania, 1719?–1806). Judge.

Richard Stockton (New Jersey, 1730–1781). Lawyer; Federalist party leader; treated badly as a prisoner of war and became an invalid.

Thomas Stone (Maryland, 1743–1787). On committee that wrote the Articles of Confederation; president of Congress during 1784.

George Taylor (Pennsylvania, 1716–1781). Iron manufacturer.

Mathew Thornton (New Hampshire, 1714–1803). Trained in medicine.

George Walton (Georgia, 1741–1804). Chief justice of Georgia; governor of Georgia.

William Whipple (New Hampshire, 1730–1785). Sea captain; merchant; judge.

William Williams (Connecticut, 1731–1811). Merchant; judge; member of Continental Congress.

James Wilson (Pennsylvania, 1742–1798). Lawyer; signer of both the Declaration of Independence and the Constitution of the United States; appointed associate justice of the United States Supreme Court by George Washington.

John Witherspoon (New Jersey, 1723–1794). Presbyterian minister; president of the College of New Jersey, which is now Princeton University.

Oliver Wolcott (Connecticut, 1726–1797). Statesman; military leader; governor of Connecticut.

George Wythe (Virginia, 1726–1806). Lawyer; judge; statesman.

President Woodruff was baptized for the signers of the Declaration of Independence and also for "fifty other eminent men, making one hundred in all."[9] He does not indicate in his journal that the other eminent men appeared to him, but he recorded their names in his journal. Following are the names of a number of the fifty eminent men, arranged alphabetically by surname, and brief biographical information about each one:[10]

---

9. *Journal of Discourses*, 19:299.

10. See also the discussion of these eminent men in Thomas E. Daniels: "I have heard that the temple work for the founding fathers of the United States has been done. Is

Lewis John Rudolph Agassis or *Jean Louis Rodolphe Agassiz* (1807–1873). Swiss zoologist; naturalist; geologist; criticized Charles Darwin's theory of evolution.

Charles Louis Napoleon Bonaparte (Napoleon III) (1808–1873). Nephew of Napoleon Bonaparte, French emperor.

Edward Bulwer-Lytton (1803–1873). English author; member of Parliament.

Henry Lord Brougham (1778–1868). Lawyer; British statesman; Lord Chancellor of Great Britain.

Robert Burns (1759–1796). Scottish poet, a favorite of Church president David O. McKay.

George Gordon Lord Byron (1788–1824). English poet.

John C. Calhoon (1782–1850). American politician; vice president of the United States under John Quincy Adams and then Andrew Jackson.

Thomas Chalmers (1780–1847). Scottish preacher; founded the Free Church of Scotland; organized relief efforts for the poor.

Henry Clay (1777–1852). American statesman; politician.

Richard Cobden (1804–1865). British statesman; manufacturer; member of Parliament.

Christopher Columbus (1451–1506). Navigator and explorer who discovered the Caribbean islands and the Americas.

Count Camillo Bonso di Cavour (1810–1861). Italian statesman and prime minister of the kingdom of Sardinia; helped to unite the kingdom of Italy.

---

that true? If so, what about the work for their families?" *Ensign*, Oct. 1991, 62. See also Vicki Jo Anderson, *The Other Eminent Men of Wilford Woodruff*, 2d ed. (Malta, Idaho: Nelson Book, 2000). Anderson wrote: "Although President Woodruff gave the number as fifty men, he recorded only forty-five names. I believe that President Woodruff's statement was not precise, but rather an estimate of the number of many men who appeared. In his journal he specified that there were one hundred men in all. The names of the signers total fifty-four; by adding the forty-five listed eminent men, the total number comes to ninety-nine. As we searched the temple records, we found in the endowments of these eminent men the name of Sir Edmund Burke, whose name was not listed in the journal. It is possible that a clerical error was made, omitting Burke's name. I am including Edmund Burke, bringing the total number of eminent men to forty-six, matching President Woodruff's journal total of one hundred. These one hundred names do not include the United States presidents whose names were also recorded in President Woodruff's journal" (2).

Daniel O'Connell (1775–1847). Irish political leader; leader of Catholic emancipation movement.

John Filpot Corran (1750–1817). Irish poet; orator; politician.

Michael Faraday (1791–1867). English physicist and chemist.

David Glascow Farragut (1801–1870). American naval officer.

Frederick II of Prussia (1712–1786). Great military leader; promoted the arts and advocated tolerance among religious groups.

David Garrick (1717–1779). British actor, known especially for his appearances in Shakespearean plays.

Edward Gibbon (1737–1794). British scholar; historian; author of *History of the Decline and Fall of the Roman Empire.*

Johann Wolfgang Goethe (1749–1832). German playwright (*Faust*); novelist; poet; scientist.

Oliver Goldsmith (1730?–1774). Irish playwright; novelist; essayist.

Henry Grattan (1746–1820). Irish politician; orator.

Alexander von Humboldt (1769–1859). German scientist; established the modern science of geography.

Washington Irving (1783–1859). American author; wrote "Rip Van Winkle" and "The Legend of Sleepy Hollow."

Thomas Jonathan "Stonewall" Jackson (1824–1863). General for the Confederacy during American Civil War.

Samuel Johnson (1709–1784). English author; lexicographer; created a dictionary of the English language that was the standard for more than a century and a half.

Benito Juarez (1806–1872). Mexican political leader responsible for economic and political reforms.

John Philip Kemble (1757–1823). British actor, especially known for his work in Shakespearean plays.

Baron Justus von Liebig (1803–1873). World-renowned German chemist.

David Livingstone (1813–1873). Scottish physician; medical missionary; explorer of Africa.

Thomas Babington Macauley (1800–1859). British writer; historian.

Horatio Lord Nelson (1758–1805). British admiral; naval hero.

George Peabody (1795–1869). American merchant; financier; philanthropist.

Hiram Powers (1805–1873). American sculptor.

Sir Joshua Reynolds (1723–1792). English portrait painter.

Frederick von Schiller (1759–1805). German playwright.

Sir Walter Scott (1771–1832). Scottish novelist, author of *Ivanhoe, Rob Roy,* and many other works.

William Henry Seward (1801–1872). Secretary of State under Abraham Lincoln; responsible for the purchase of Alaska from Russia.

George Stephenson (1781–1848). British engineer; inventor of the miner's lamp, the alarm clock, and an efficient locomotive.

William Makepeace Thackeray (1811–1863). English novelist.

Amerigo Vespucci (1451?–1512). Italian explorer; in 1497 discovered the American mainland, which was named for him.

Daniel Webster (1782–1852). American orator; statesman; lawyer; politician.

John Wesley (1703–1791). Church of England clergyman; founder of the Methodist Church.

William Wordsworth (1770–1850). English poet.

President Woodruff recorded: "When Br McAllister had Baptized me for the 100 Names I Baptized him for 21, including Gen Washington & his forefathers and all the Presidents of the United States that were not in my list. Except Buchannan Van Buren & Grant."[11]

In addition to the work for the signers of the Declaration of Independence and the "fifty other eminent men," President Woodruff oversaw the work of baptisms for the dead on behalf of "seventy of the eminent women of the world." He recorded: "Sister Lucy Bigelow Young went forth into the font and was baptized for Martha Washington and her family and seventy (70) of the eminent women of the world. I called upon all the brethren & sisters who were present to assist in getting Endowments for those that we had been baptized for to day."[12]

The names of many of the seventy eminent women, listed alphabetically by surname and with brief biographical information, are as follows:

Marie Antoinette (1755–1793). Queen of Louis XVI of France.

Jean Armour (1767–1834). Wife of Robert Burns.

---

11. Journal, Aug. 21, 1877. United States president Ulysses S. Grant had not yet died when these baptisms were performed.
12. Journal, Aug. 21, 1877.

APPENDIX

Jane Austen (1775–1817). English novelist.

Mary Ball (1708–1789). Mother of George Washington.

Sarah Barnard (1800–1879). Wife of Michael Faraday.

Charlotte Brontë (1816–1855). English novelist.

Felecia Dorothea Browne (1793–1835). English poet.

Elizabeth Barrett Browning (1806–1861). English poet.

Frances Burney (1752–1840). English writer and playwright.

Jane Butler (1699–1728). First wife of Augustine Washington, the father of George Washington.

Martha Caldwell (1730–1802). Wife of Patrick Calhoun, who fought in the Revolutionary War.

Eleanor Calvert (1750–1811). Wife of John Parke Custis, son of Martha Washington and stepson of George Washington.

Charlotte Margaret Carpenter (1770–1826). Wife of Sir Walter Scott.

Charlotte Corday (1768–1793). French patriot.

Sarah Creagh (1755–1844). Wife of John Curran, Irish orator; lawyer; judge; politician.

Martha Parke Custis. (1777–1854) Step-granddaughter of George Washington.

Martha Dandridge (1731–1802). Wife of George Washington.

Rachel Donelson (1767–1828). Wife of Andrew Jackson.

Elizabeth Dyke. Actress; wife of Thomas Moore.

Abigail Eastman (1739–1816). Mother of Daniel Webster.

Mary Ann Eden (1785–1865). Wife of Henry Lord Brougham.

Maria Edgeworth (1767/68–1849). English novelist; wrote about life in Ireland.

Anne Fairfax (1728–1761). Wife of Lawrence Washington, half-brother of George Washington.

Henrietta Fitzgerald. Wife of Henry Grattan.

Grace Fletcher (1781–1828). Wife of Daniel Webster.

Sarah Ford. Mother of Samuel Johnson.

Sarah Margaret Fuller (1810–1850). American journalist; reformer for women's rights.

Elizabeth Gurney (1780–1845). English social reformer.

Fanny Henderson (1768–1805). Wife of George Stephenson.

Matilda Hoffman (1791–1809). Fiancée of Washington Irving.

Lydia Huntley (1791–1865). American author.

Mary Hutchinson (1770–1859). Wife of William Wordsworth.

Margarita Maza de Juarez (1826–1871). Wife of Benito Juarez.

Elinor Junkin (1825–1854). Wife of "Stonewall" Jackson.

Emily Chubbuch Judson (1817–1854). American author.

Emily Lamb (1787–1869). Wife of Lord Palmerston, British prime minister.

Letitia Elizabeth Landon (1802–1838). English poet.

Charlotte von Lingefeld (1766–1826). Poet; writer; wife of Fredrick Schiller.

Sarah van Brugh Livingston (1756–1802). Wife of John Jay, president of the Continental Congress.

Francis Locke (Osgood) (1811–1850). American poet.

Anna Isabella Milbanke (1792–1860). Wife of George Gordon Lord Byron.

Mary Russell Milford (1787–1855). English novelist; playwright.

Hannah Moore (1745–1833). English author.

Lady Sidney Morgan (1783?–1859). Irish novelist.

Anna Murphy (1794–1860). Irish archaeologist; author.

Jane Mary Nugent (1734–1812). Wife of Edmund Burke, Irish statesman; author; orator; political theorist; philosopher.

Mary O'Connell (1775–1836). Wife of Daniel O'Connell.

Catherine Pakenham (1773–1831). Wife of Arthur Wellesley, Duke of Wellington.

Countess Demetrius Parepa (1815–1870). Wife of Demetrius Parepa and mother of Euphrosyne Parepa.

Euphrosyne Parepa (1836–1874). Opera singer.

Dorothy "Dolley" Madison (1768?–1849). Wife of James Madison.

Catherine Maria Sedgwick (1789–1867). American novelist.

Isabella Shawe (1818–1894). Wife of William Makepeace Thackeray.

Sarah Kemble Siddons (1755–1831). English actress.

Martha Wayles Skelton (1748–1782). Wife of Thomas Jefferson.

Abigail Smith (1744–1818). Wife of John Adams; mother of John Quincy Adams, sixth U.S. president.

Mary Fairfax Summerville. Scottish mathematician.

Empress Maria Theresa (1717–1780). Mother of Marie Antoinette.

Eva Maria Veigel (1724–1822). Wife of David Garrick.

Christiane Vulpius (1765–1816). Wife of Johann Wolfgang Goethe.

Mildred Warner (1671–1701). Mother of Augustine Washington.

After baptisms for the dead had been performed on behalf of the signers of the Declaration of Independence and the other eminent men and women by President Woodruff, additional sacred ordinances were conducted for a number of the Founding Fathers and others. President Ezra Taft Benson wrote, "President George Washington was ordained a high priest at that time. You will also be interested to know that, according to Wilford Woodruff's journal, John Wesley, Benjamin Franklin, and Christopher Columbus were also ordained high priests at that time."[13]

13. *Teachings of Ezra Taft Benson*, 604.

Sources Cited

Adam, Jennie Lee, comp. "Mary Elizabeth Rollins Lightner, 1818–1913." Archives of The Church of Jesus Christ of Latter-day Saints, Salt Lake City, Utah.

"Alexander Neibaur." *Utah Genealogical and Historical Magazine,* Apr. 1914, 61–63.

Allen, Leslie C. *Ezekiel 20–48.* Vol. 29 of Word Biblical Commentary. Dallas: Word Books, 1990.

Andersen, Neil L. "What Thinks Christ of Me?" *Ensign,* May 2012, 111–14.

Anderson, Richard Lloyd. *Investigating the Book of Mormon Witnesses.* Salt Lake City: Deseret Book, 1981.

Barrett, Ivan J. *Joseph Smith and the Restoration.* Provo, Utah: Brigham Young University Press, 1967.

Bateman, Eric D., comp. and ed. *The Prophets Have Spoken.* 3 vols. Salt Lake City: Deseret Book, 1999.

Baugh, Alexander L. "Parting the Veil: Joseph Smith's Seventy-six Documented Visionary Experiences." In Welch and Carlson, *Opening the Heavens,* 265–326.

Benson, Ezra Taft. *Come unto Christ.* Salt Lake City: Deseret Book, 1983.

———. "To the Children of the Church." *Friend,* June 1989, 2–5.

Benson, Ezra Taft. *The Teachings of Ezra Taft Benson.* Edited by Reed A. Benson. Salt Lake City: Bookcraft, 1988.

Best-Loved Stories of the LDS People. Vol. 1. Edited by Jack M. Lyon, Linda Ririe Gundry, and Jay A. Parry. Salt Lake City: Deseret Book, 1997.

"Biography of Nathan Pratt." *Times and Seasons* 5 (15 Jan. 1844): 414–15.

Boice, James M. *Genesis 1–11.* Vol. 1 of *Genesis: An Expositional Commentary.* Grand Rapids, Mich.: Baker Books, 1998.

Brown, Francis, S. R. Driver, and Charles A. Briggs, eds. *A Hebrew and*

English Lexicon of the Old Testament. Translated by Edward Robinson. Oxford: Clarendon, 1977.

Brown, Matthew B., and Paul Thomas Smith. *Symbols in Stone: Symbolism on the Early Temples of the Restoration.* American Fork, Utah: Covenant Communications, 1997.

Burgess, Harrison. "Sketch of a Well-Spent Life." In *Labors in the Vineyard: Twelfth Book of the Faith-Promoting Series.* Salt Lake City: Juvenile Instructor Office, 1884.

Cannon, George Q. "A Dream." *Juvenile Instructor* 32, no. 21 (Nov. 1, 1897): 656.

———. "The Angels Who Visit Us." *Juvenile Instructor* 26 (Jan. 15, 1891): 53–54.

———. "God's Care for All His Creations." *Juvenile Instructor* 24, no. 2 (Jan. 15, 1889): 36–37.

———. *Gospel Truth: Discourses and Writings of President George Q. Cannon.* Compiled and edited by Jerreld L. Newquist. 2 vols. Salt Lake City: Zion's Book Store, 1957.

Clawson, Rudger. Conference Report, April 1925, 60–64.

Cowley, Matthias F. *Wilford Woodruff: History of His Life and Labors.* Salt Lake City: Bookcraft, 1964.

Dahl, Larry E., and Donald Q. Cannon, eds. *Encyclopedia of Joseph Smith's Teachings.* Salt Lake City: Bookcraft, 1997.

Davis, R. Dean. *The Heavenly Court Judgment of Revelation 4–5.* Lanham, Md.: University Press of America, 1992.

Ehat, Andrew F., and Lyndon W. Cook, comps. and eds. *The Words of Joseph Smith.* Provo, Utah: BYU Religious Studies Center, 1980.

Eyring, Henry B. "O Ye That Embark." *Ensign,* Nov. 2008, 57–59.

———. "Walk in the Light." *Ensign,* May 2008, 123–25.

Faust, James E. "How Near to the Angels." *Ensign,* May 1998, 95–97.

———. "A Royal Priesthood." *Ensign,* May 2006, 50–53.

First Presidency [Heber J. Grant, J. Reuben Clark Jr., and David O. McKay]. Conference Report, Apr. 1942, 88–97.

"A Friend of the Helpless Dead." *Relief Society Magazine* 4 (Sept. 1917): 483–86.

Gates, Susa Young, and Leah D. Widtsoe. *The Life Story of Brigham Young.* New York: Macmillan, 1930.

Gates, Susa Young. "Temple Workers' Excursion." *Young Woman's Journal* 5 (1894): 512–13.

Gibbs, Eliza. Autobiography. In *Writings of Early Latter-day Saints.* Salt Lake City: Deseret Book, 1980, eBook edition.

Grant, Heber J. *Gospel Standards.* Compiled by G. Homer Durham. Salt Lake City: Improvement Era, 1969.

Haight, David B. "Come to the House of the Lord." *Ensign,* May 1992, 15–17.

Hales, Robert D. "The Covenant of Baptism: To Be in the Kingdom and of the Kingdom." *Ensign,* Nov. 2000, 6–8.

Hamilton, Victor P. *The Book of Genesis.* Grand Rapids, Mich.: W. B. Eerdmans, 1990.

Harper, Steven C. "A Pentecost and Endowment Indeed": Six Eyewitness Accounts of the Kirtland Temple Experience." In Welch and Carlson, *Opening the Heavens,* 327–71.

Hinckley, Gordon B. "Stay the Course—Keep the Faith." *Ensign,* Nov. 1995, 70–72.

———. "This Glorious Easter Morn." *Ensign,* May 1996, 65–67.

———. "To the Boys and to the Men." *Ensign,* Nov. 1998, 51–53.

Holland, Jeffrey R. "An Ensign to the Nations." *Ensign,* May 2011, 111–13.

———. "For a Wise Purpose." *Ensign,* Jan. 1996, 16–17.

———. *However Long and Hard the Road.* Salt Lake City: Deseret Book, 2002.

———. "Lessons from Liberty Jail." *Ensign,* Sept. 2009, 26–33.

———. "The Ministry of Angels." *Ensign,* Nov. 2008, 29–31.

———. "The Peaceable Things of the Kingdom." *Ensign,* Nov. 1996, 82–84.

———. "Place No More for the Enemy of My Soul." *Ensign,* May 2010, 44–46.

Holzapfel, Jeni Broberg, and Richard Neitzel Holzapfel. *A Woman's View: Helen Mar Whitney's Reminiscences of Early Church History.* Provo, Utah: BYU Religious Studies Center, 1997.

Hymns of The Church of Jesus Christ of Latter-day Saints. Salt Lake City: The Church of Jesus Christ of Latter-day Saints, 1985.

Jenson, Andrew. *Latter-day Saint Biographical Encyclopedia.* 4 vols. Salt Lake City: Andrew Jenson History, 1901–36.

Jessee, Dean C., comp. and ed. *The Papers of Joseph Smith.* Vol. 1. Salt Lake City: Deseret Book, 1989.

Journal of Discourses. 26 vols. London: Latter-day Saints' Book Depot, 1854–86.

Kimball, Spencer W. "The Cause Is Just and Worthy." *Ensign,* May 1974, 118–19.

———. *The Teachings of Spencer W. Kimball.* Edited by Edward L. Kimball. Salt Lake City: Bookcraft, 1982.

———. "The Things of Eternity—Stand We in Jeopardy?" *Ensign,* Jan. 1977, 2–7.

Koehler, Ludwig, and Walter Baumgartner. *The Hebrew and Aramaic Lexicon of the Old Testament.* 2 vols. Leiden: Brill, 2002.

LDS Beliefs: A Doctrinal Reference. Edited by Robert L. Millet, Camille Fronk Olson, Andrew C. Skinner, and Brent L. Top. Salt Lake City: Deseret Book, 2011.

Lee, Harold B. "The Influence and Responsibility of Women." *Relief Society Magazine* 51 (Feb. 1964): 84–89.

———. *Stand Ye in Holy Places: Selected Sermons and Writings of President Harold B. Lee.* Salt Lake City: Deseret Book, 1974.

———. "Stand Ye in Holy Places." *Ensign,* July 1973, 121–24.

———. *The Teachings of Harold B. Lee.* Edited by Clyde J. Williams. Salt Lake City: Bookcraft, 1996.

"Letter No. 4." *Latter Day Saints' Messenger and Advocate* 1, no. 5 (Feb. 1835): 65–67.

Ludlow, Daniel H., ed. *Encyclopedia of Mormonism.* 4 vols. New York: Macmillan, 1992.

Matthews, Robert J. *Selected Writings of Robert J. Matthews.* Salt Lake City: Deseret Book, 1999.

Maxwell, Neal A. "From the Beginning." *Ensign,* Oct. 1993, 18–20.

———. "The Seventh Commandment: A Shield." *Ensign,* Nov. 2001, 78–80.

McAllister, John D. T. *Contributor* 16 (1894–95): 145–48.

McConkie, Bruce R. *Mormon Doctrine.* 2d ed. Salt Lake City: Bookcraft, 1966.

———. "Stand Independent above All Other Creatures." *Ensign,* May 1979, 92–93.

McConkie, Joseph Fielding, and Craig J. Ostler. *Revelations of the Restoration.* Salt Lake City: Deseret Book, 2000.

McConkie, Mark L. *Remembering Joseph: Personal Recollections of Those Who Knew the Prophet Joseph Smith.* Salt Lake City: Deseret Book, 2003.

McConkie, Oscar W. *Angels.* Salt Lake City: Deseret Book, 1975.

McKay, David O. Conference Report, Oct. 1968, 84–88.

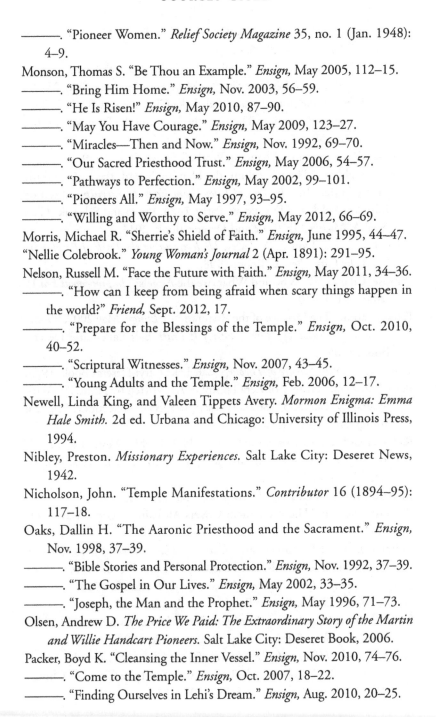

———. "Pioneer Women." *Relief Society Magazine* 35, no. 1 (Jan. 1948): 4–9.

Monson, Thomas S. "Be Thou an Example." *Ensign,* May 2005, 112–15.

———. "Bring Him Home." *Ensign,* Nov. 2003, 56–59.

———. "He Is Risen!" *Ensign,* May 2010, 87–90.

———. "May You Have Courage." *Ensign,* May 2009, 123–27.

———. "Miracles—Then and Now." *Ensign,* Nov. 1992, 69–70.

———. "Our Sacred Priesthood Trust." *Ensign,* May 2006, 54–57.

———. "Pathways to Perfection." *Ensign,* May 2002, 99–101.

———. "Pioneers All." *Ensign,* May 1997, 93–95.

———. "Willing and Worthy to Serve." *Ensign,* May 2012, 66–69.

Morris, Michael R. "Sherrie's Shield of Faith." *Ensign,* June 1995, 44–47.

"Nellie Colebrook." *Young Woman's Journal* 2 (Apr. 1891): 291–95.

Nelson, Russell M. "Face the Future with Faith." *Ensign,* May 2011, 34–36.

———. "How can I keep from being afraid when scary things happen in the world?" *Friend,* Sept. 2012, 17.

———. "Prepare for the Blessings of the Temple." *Ensign,* Oct. 2010, 40–52.

———. "Scriptural Witnesses." *Ensign,* Nov. 2007, 43–45.

———. "Young Adults and the Temple." *Ensign,* Feb. 2006, 12–17.

Newell, Linda King, and Valeen Tippets Avery. *Mormon Enigma: Emma Hale Smith.* 2d ed. Urbana and Chicago: University of Illinois Press, 1994.

Nibley, Preston. *Missionary Experiences.* Salt Lake City: Deseret News, 1942.

Nicholson, John. "Temple Manifestations." *Contributor* 16 (1894–95): 117–18.

Oaks, Dallin H. "The Aaronic Priesthood and the Sacrament." *Ensign,* Nov. 1998, 37–39.

———. "Bible Stories and Personal Protection." *Ensign,* Nov. 1992, 37–39.

———. "The Gospel in Our Lives." *Ensign,* May 2002, 33–35.

———. "Joseph, the Man and the Prophet." *Ensign,* May 1996, 71–73.

Olsen, Andrew D. *The Price We Paid: The Extraordinary Story of the Martin and Willie Handcart Pioneers.* Salt Lake City: Deseret Book, 2006.

Packer, Boyd K. "Cleansing the Inner Vessel." *Ensign,* Nov. 2010, 74–76.

———. "Come to the Temple." *Ensign,* Oct. 2007, 18–22.

———. "Finding Ourselves in Lehi's Dream." *Ensign,* Aug. 2010, 20–25.

———. "The Gift of the Holy Ghost: What Every Member Should Know." *Ensign,* Aug. 2006, 46–52.

———. "How Does the Spirit Speak to Us?" *New Era,* Feb. 2010, 2–3.

———. "I Will Remember Your Sins No More." *Ensign,* May 2006, 25–27.

———. *Mine Errand from the Lord.* Salt Lake City: Deseret Book, 2008.

———. "Personal Revelation: The Gift, the Test, and the Promise." *Ensign,* Nov. 1994, 59–62.

———. "Revelation in a Changing World." *Ensign,* Nov. 1989, 14–16.

Parry, Donald W. "The Cherubim, the Flaming Sword, the Path, and the Tree of Life." In *The Tree of Life: From Eden to Eternity,* edited by John W. Welch and Donald W. Parry, 1–24. Provo and Salt Lake City: Neal A. Maxwell Institute and Deseret Book, 2011.

Parry, Jay A., and Donald W. Parry. *Understanding the Book of Revelation.* Salt Lake City: Deseret Book, 1998.

Penrose, Charles W. "Who and What Are the Angels?" *Improvement Era* 15 (Aug. 1912): 950.

Perry, L. Tom. "The Message of the Restoration." *Ensign,* May 2007, 85–88.

Pratt, Parley P. *Autobiography of Parley P. Pratt.* Salt Lake City: Deseret Book, 1985.

———. *Key to the Science of Theology.* Salt Lake City: Deseret Book, 1973.

Pulsipher, Zera. "History of Zera Pulsipher As Written by Himself." Autobiography (ca. 1803–1862). Typescript, Special Collections, Brigham Young University, Provo, Utah.

Rad, Gerhard von. *Genesis: A Commentary.* Philadelphia: Westminster, 1961.

"Report of Elders Orson Pratt and Joseph F. Smith," *Millennial Star* 40 (Dec. 9, 1878): 771–74.

Richards, Franklin D. *Deseret Weekly* 46 (Mar. 18, 1893): 390.

Richards, Kent F. "The Atonement Covers All Pain." *Ensign,* May 2011, 15–17.

Roberts, B. H. *A Comprehensive History of The Church of Jesus Christ of Latter-day Saints.* 6 vols. Salt Lake City: Deseret News, 1930.

———. *The Life of John Taylor.* Salt Lake City: Bookcraft, 1963.

Smith, Hyrum G. Conference Report, Oct. 1928, 81–82.

Smith, Hyrum M., ed. *From Prophet to Son: Advice of Joseph F. Smith to His Missionary Sons.* Salt Lake City: Deseret Book, 1981.

Smith, Joseph. *History of The Church of Jesus Christ of Latter-day Saints.* Edited by B. H. Roberts. 2d ed. rev. 7 vols. Salt Lake City: The Church of Jesus Christ of Latter-day Saints, 1932–51.

————. *Teachings of the Prophet Joseph Smith.* Selected by Joseph Fielding Smith. Salt Lake City: Deseret Book, 1976.

Smith, Joseph F. Conference Report, April 1916, 1–8.

————. *Gospel Doctrine.* Salt Lake City: Deseret Book, 1978.

Smith, Joseph Fielding. *Answers to Gospel Questions.* 5 vols. Salt Lake City: Deseret Book, 1957–66.

————. *Church History and Modern Revelation.* 4 vols. Salt Lake City: Council of the Twelve Apostles of the Church of Jesus Christ of Latter-day Saints, 1947–50.

————. *Doctrines of Salvation.* Compiled by Bruce R. McConkie. 3 vols. Salt Lake City: Bookcraft, 1954–66.

————, comp. *The Life of Joseph F. Smith.* Salt Lake City: Deseret News, 1969.

————. "Out of the Darkness." *Ensign,* May 1971, 2–4.

Snow, Erastus. "Sketch Book." Nov. 1818–Jan. 2, 1838, Typescript, Special Collections, Brigham Young University, Provo, Utah.

"Spiritual Manifestations in the Manti Temple." *Millennial Star* 50 (1888): 520–23.

Stevenson, Edward. "The Thirteenth Witness to the Plates of the Book of Mormon." *Millennial Star* 55 (1893): 214–16.

Stuy, Brian H., ed. *Collected Discourses Delivered by President Wilford Woodruff, His Two Counselors, the Twelve Apostles, and Others.* 5 vols. Burbank, Cal.: B. H. S. Publishing, 1987–92.

Talmage, James E. *Articles of Faith.* Salt Lake City: Deseret Book, 1977.

————. *Millennial Star* 55 (July 10, 1893): 445–49.

Tanner, N. Eldon. "Warnings from Outer Space." *Ensign,* Jan. 1973, 26–29.

Taylor, John. *The Gospel Kingdom.* Edited by G. Homer Durham. Salt Lake City: Bookcraft, 1964.

Tullidge, Edward W. *The Women of Mormondom.* New York: Tullidge & Crandall, 1877.

Uchtdorf, Dieter F. "Hold on a Little Longer." *Ensign,* Jan. 2010, 4–8.

————. "We Are Doing a Great Work and Cannot Come Down." *Ensign,* May 2009, 59–62.

————. "Your Happily Ever After." *Ensign,* May 2010, 124–27.

Walker, Charles L. *Diary of Charles Lowell Walker.* Edited by A. Karl Larson and Katharine Miles Larson. 2 vols. Logan: Utah State University Press, 1980.

Waltke, Bruce K., and Cathi J. Fredricks. *Genesis: A Commentary.* Grand Rapids, Mich.: Zondervan, 2001.

Watson, Elden J., comp. *Manuscript History of Brigham Young 1846–1847.* Salt Lake City: Elden J. Watson, 1971.

Welch, John W., and Erick B. Carlson, eds. *Opening the Heavens: Accounts of Divine Manifestations, 1820–1844.* Provo, Utah: Brigham Young University Press; Salt Lake City: Deseret Book, 2005.

Whitney, Helen Mar. "Some Serious Reflections." *Woman's Exponent* 17 (Oct. 15, 1888): 73–74.

Whitney, Orson F. *History of Utah.* Vol. 4. Salt Lake City: George Q. Cannon & Sons, 1904.

———. *The Life of Heber C. Kimball.* Salt Lake City: Bookcraft, 1992.

———. *Saturday Night Thoughts.* Salt Lake City: Deseret News, 1927.

———. *Through Memory's Halls: The Life Story of Orson F. Whitney.* Independence, Mo.: Zion's Printing and Publishing, 1930.

Widtsoe, John A. *Evidences and Reconciliations.* Salt Lake City: Bookcraft, 1960.

———. *Gospel Interpretations.* Salt Lake City: Bookcraft, 1947.

———. *A Rational Theology.* Salt Lake City: Deseret Book, 1965.

Woodruff, Wilford. Conference Report, April 1880, 6–14.

———. *Deseret Weekly* 41 (Oct. 11, 1890): 517; 53 (Oct. 24, 1896): 577; 53 (Nov. 7, 1896): 642.

———. *The Discourses of Wilford Woodruff.* Edited by G. Homer Durham. Salt Lake City: Bookcraft, 1990.

———. *Leaves from My Journal.* American Fork, Utah: Covenant Communications, 2005.

———. Wilford Woodruff Journals and Papers, 1828–1898. Church History Library, The Church of Jesus Christ of Latter-day Saints, Salt Lake City, Utah.

Young, Brigham. *Brigham Young.* Teachings of Presidents of the Church series. Salt Lake City: The Church of Jesus Christ of Latter-day Saints, 1997.

———. *Discourses of Brigham Young.* Compiled by John A. Widtsoe. Salt Lake City: Deseret Book, 1941.

Young, John R. *Memoirs of John R. Young: Utah Pioneer, 1847.* Salt Lake City: Deseret News, 1920.

INDEX

Index